Escape to Miracles

An autobiography about abuse, co-dependency, alcoholism, and taking responsibility for one's own healing and spirituality.

By I. H. Wendland

In order to protect the anonymity of the people mentioned in this book, other names were used when necessary.

A special Thank You to Pat Vaughn, Psychologist and to my friends and family for the encouragement and support they gave me to write my story.

Credits:
Typing .... Gina Bourdeau
Cover Art .... Myron Wendland
Editing .... Theonilla Troumbly

First printing, November, 1994.

Copyright © 1994 by I. H. Wendland, P.O. Box 2142, North Mankato, MN 56002. All rights reserved.

ISBN 0-9643823-0-X

Dedication

I dedicate this book to my grandfather, our sponsors, and my husband. Without the unconditional love they gave me, I may not be who I am today. To God, my Heavenly Father, who loved me so much that He gave me all of you to help me survive, learn, grow, and become what He meant for me to be.

Table of Contents

PREFACE
INTRODUCTION
CHAPTER 1: GERMANY
  1 First Memory 11
  2 A Difficult Beginning 12
  3 The Homecoming 13
  4 Scarlet Fever 16
  5 My Grandparents 18
  6 Field of Daisies 23
  7 Time for School 23
  8 The City 29
  9 The Dream 36
CHAPTER 2: GOING TO AMERICA
  10 Ocean Voyage 39
  11 A New Culture 44
  12 A Hamlet 47
  13 Trip Out West. 53
  14 Taking Control 55
  15 Bible Camp 63
  16 Ambivalence 64
CHAPTER 3: DECISIONS
  17 On My Own 71
  18 California 72
  19 Physical or Mental 80
  20 Arizona 84

CHAPTER 4: BETTER OFF WITHOUT ME
21 Coming Home 87
22 Mankato 90
23 Suicide Attempt 92
24 Assembly of God Church 100
25 Our Own Home 105

CHAPTER 5: ALONE WITH CHILDREN
26 Divorced 111
27 Our Trip to Germany 113
28 Abandonment 118
29 A Hint of Sanity 124

CHAPTER 6: A NEW BEGINNING
30 God's Grace 129
31 Healing Begins 131
32 Living Reality 136
33 My Arrogance 146
34 He Sent an Angel 149
35 Rigorous Honesty 154
36 Becoming Assertive 157

CHAPTER 7: DISCOVERING LOVE
37 A Friend and Partner 163
38 Primeval Therapy 174
39 Trip to Florida 177
40 Power Without Responsibility 180

CHAPTER 8: REVELATION AND RESOLVE
41 Feelings of Abandonment Manifested 185
42 Detaching with Love 191
43 Rewards 194

SUMMARY 203

Preface

Our memories and feelings are our interpretations of events that took place in each of our lifetimes. They shape us and teach us how to deal with those around us, and life in general.

I believe we all start out exactly the same. We are souls, born into a body. What makes you different from me, it seems, are three variables:

1. No two people, even within a family unit, are ever treated exactly the same; we all have our own distinct experiences.

2. We choose to remember what happens to us by our own way of interpreting the facts. Twins who are raised in the same environment will interpret that environment each in his or her own way, individually shaping memories. Those memories will affect each of them by either helping or hindering him or her in adulthood.

3. It is our soul with which we decide what to do with our experiences. It is that force within each of us from which we can gather strength.

I firmly believe that the quality of our lives is influenced much more by our souls than by any experience or environment. It has been a very difficult road which has brought me to such a conclusion.

I believe that each of our souls is a part of a greater soul in the universe from which we come, and to which we shall return. What we do during our brief stay here on earth is left completely up to us. We can choose to connect to that greater soul and become what we were meant to be, or we can choose to go our own way.

This book is about taking responsibility for my own life and happiness. It is about connecting with my Higher Power, whom I choose to call God, so I can receive His power to change. It is about the realization that He has always been there for me, even when I did not acknowledge Him. It is also a story of abuse, survival, love, hate, forgiveness, spirituality, and healing.

For the past twenty years, I have had a haunting feeling for the need to write about my experiences, strengths, and hopes. The feeling has not left me alone. Each time I have thought seriously about allowing myself to be so vulnerable as to let you know what happened to me, how I dealt with it, and where I am today, my heart pounds and my stomach feels like a batch of butterflies has invaded it. The time was not right, until now.

To those of you who have been abused, I applaud your strength to survive so that you can grow to be who you were meant to be. I know of your deep knowledge that human beings can hurt your body but cannot touch your soul.

I pray for your determination to stop abuse whenever and wherever you may find it. That, ultimately, will truly be your healing.

Introduction

In March of 1945, my mother, grandparents, great grandmother, sister and I lived in a two-bedroom apartment in Waldenburg, East Germany. An aunt and uncle and their daughter lived in the same building in a separate apartment. My father was not with us because he was a soldier in the German Air Force.

My grandfather was the only person who was able to work. He supported everyone with his earnings from working in the coal mines.

In May, when World War II was declared officially over, the city was in chaos because no one was in charge of anything. Food was very difficult to come by. Since my grandfather worked in the coal mines, he had coal he could trade for food. Potatoes were the only food somewhat in abundance so my family's main diet was potatoes.

My great-grandmother left Waldenburg and moved to Reichenbach because it was too hard for my grandfather to support everyone. My mother and sister joined her in November of 1945, and I was left behind with my grandparents and aunt.

In March of 1946, I was reunited with my mother and sister in Reichenbach. My grandparents were not allowed to leave Waldenburg because the Poles had taken over the city and forced my grandfather to continue working in the coal mines.

In April, the Poles took over Reichenbach. They threw us, along with many other families, out of our homes. They shipped us out by train to West Germany. My family ended up in a small town called Marienfeld. It was not until 1950 that my grandparents were finally allowed to leave Waldenburg and join us in Marienfeld.

CHAPTER 1 - GERMANY

1 First Memory

Huddled in the thickly forested hills on a dark, damp, and cold night were my grandfather, grandmother, mother and a few other relatives. My grandfather held me in his arms to keep me warm. He had a bottle of milk inside his jacket for me. Fear was on each face–fear so great you could feel it hanging in the air. No one talked and I felt that if I cried, I would put everyone in terrible danger. In the distance, I heard footsteps–many footsteps. The louder they became, the stronger the fear. Then the dream stops.

I talked to my mother about this dream because it resurfaced periodically during the course of my life, and I wanted to know if she could shed any light on it. She looked at me as if in shock, and told me that in 1945, our family hid in the hills outside of Waldenburg, Germany because the Russian soldiers were reported to be coming our way. They were known to rape women and children and take whatever they wanted. When the soldiers finally left town, we went back to our home. They had looted the town of everything they could carry. The war was considered over as far as the rest of the world was concerned, but it was not over for many German people. My mother said I was only six months old when this occurred so I could not possibly have remembered it. My subconscious did remember, however, and it reminded me of the incident via the dream. Since talking with my mother about it nine years ago, I have not had the dream again.

2 A Difficult Beginning

My mother told me that at an age of two weeks, I contracted Whooping Cough. The doctor said I would not survive and as she could not bear to watch me die, my mother turned me over to my great aunt. However, there was a woman on a farm who was known to cure all kinds of diseases with herb and spice concoctions so my grandfather went to her to see if she could help. She gave him a mixture to give to me, but she said she did not know if it would work since I was so young. It might do more harm than good! Since there was nothing else to try, they gave it to me and within days I was getting better.

I was constantly sick my first year of life. The main reason was that the food a baby needs to grow strong and healthy was just not available to my family. Much of my diet consisted of water and flour mixed together, but at least I had something in my stomach. Whenever they could get milk for me, they would. That meant, however, my grandfather and my mother often risked their lives to get it. No one was allowed out after dark. If one was caught, the chances of being shot were good. My grandfather worked ten to fourteen hours a day. Then, in the middle of the night, he or my mother walked from farm to farm and asked for milk. Sometimes they were given some, but most of the time they were turned away.

My grandfather was the only member of the family who was allowed to work at the time. He worked in the coal mines. Pay was done by a voucher system and it was not enough to feed oneself, much less an entire family. One night when he had gone to get milk, he was stopped by a Russian soldier. The soldier asked him what he was doing and grandfather told him. The soldier went with him to the nearest farmhouse and, at gunpoint, ordered the farmer to give my grandfather all the milk he needed. I tell you this because we sometimes seem to forget that even in the worst of times, there are compassionate people in every culture, race, or neighborhood.

3 The Homecoming

During the war, my father had been taken as a prisoner, and he was taken to a POW Camp in Italy. He was released in 1947 and shipped back to Germany. My mother told me many things about my father. He was a wonderful, kind man and he and I would certainly get along well. I used to look at his picture and wish for him to come home. I was very excited the day he finally did come home.

We were living in a rented room on a farm. The room was approximately ten feet by twenty feet. It held a double bed, a small table with chairs, my crib, a small cook stove, and a small closet. My grandparents were no longer with us because we had been forced out of our home in the East, and they were not allowed to come with us. The day my father came home, I ran to him with open arms. He slapped me and I fell backwards into the wall behind me, ending up on the floor. I felt confused, shocked, and asked myself what I had done wrong. I could not cry even though I wanted to. I just kept looking at my father wondering what was wrong with me. Why had he hit me? I felt fear. I remember thinking, "what do I do now? Do I approach him cautiously, or do I just stay away?" I was two years old and I remember my thoughts and feelings about that day as if it had happened yesterday. The setup for what was to happen in the future had begun. A family victimizer sets up his victim emotionally and psychologically. I did not know it then, but I know how it works today and why.

My mother and father fought all the time. I wanted to hide when they yelled at each other, but there was nowhere to go in that small room. I would be put in the crib when they started fighting and I would lay down, cover myself totally, and pretend as hard as I could that I was somewhere else. Sometimes I actually succeeded and stopped hearing the yelling. I created a world for myself away from reality. It worked only until I could hear my mother cry out in pain. Then I screamed or cried to get my father's attention away from her. I was trying to protect her and ended up putting myself in the way. During this period of time, I saw my mother with black and blue eyes, bloody noses, and at one time, a severely injured left arm. I was petrified every night my father walked through the door, wondering what would happen that night. I became very hyperactive, which only made matters worse. No matter how good I tried to be, I was accused of doing something wrong by my father. I believed my father did not want me around.

My mother was gone a lot because she was working. When she worked in the evenings, my father had the responsibility of taking care of me but he often left me alone while he went drinking. There were many nights when I woke up and no one was with me. The room was dark and I was in my crib.

After one particular night when I was left in the care of my father, my mother tried to wake me the next morning. I could not fully wake up. She pulled back my covers and I heard her gasp. She turned to my father and asked what happened. My father got up, looked into the crib where I was laying and said he did not know. My pajamas and bed sheets had blood on them. I can still hear my mother as she tried to wake me. There was panic in her voice. I heard her but I could not respond. It was like being in a tunnel between two worlds. I heard my mother say she was going to get a doctor. My father refused to let her go. When they started to fight, I forced myself to wake up. I kept thinking that I had to wake up or he would kill her. As soon as I awoke, my father said, "See, she is just fine." That night before was the first time my father sexually molested me. I was between two and three years old.

After that night I started to wet the bed. Each time I did, my father beat me so hard that I had welts on my bottom and then he made me sit on a glass nightpot for hours. One day after I had wet the bed, he took me over his knees and when he started beating me, I consciously decided to urinate on him. He threw me off and never again took me over his knees to hit me.

The people who owned the farm where we rented our room were warm and wonderful people. I called the man Uncle Rolf. He let me be anywhere I wanted to be on the farm. Many times he put me on his plow horse and let me ride. At supper time, I would tell my mother that I had to go to the bathroom. The bathroom we used was on the other side of the farmhouse kitchen, so I had to walk through Uncle Rolf's kitchen while they were eating. They always asked me to stay and eat with them, which was the reason I told my mother I had to go to the bathroom in the first place. Besides, this way I would not have to be with my father and they had better food than we did. I did this as often as I could possibly get away with it.

One night, I awoke to a terrible thunderstorm and I was alone. I cried and screamed because I was scared. Uncle Rolf came to our door and tried to calm me down. The door was locked so all he could do was try to soothe me by talking to me. Each time the lightning flashed and the thunder crashed, I screamed even louder. Then I saw my father's silhouette in our window as he walked by. Fear gripped me. I lay down and tried to stop crying, pretending I was asleep. I heard our landlord angrily tell my father how I had been crying and screaming. He warned my father not to leave me alone again. My father came in and beat me. All the while he was beating me, he warned me not to cry. I did not cry.

4 Scarlet Fever

I have a sister who is almost four years older than me. She did not live with us. She was being raised by our great-grandmother. My great-grandmother did not like me. She did not want my mother to have any more children after my sister was born. Whenever I was around her, I felt her disapproval by the way she ignored me. When she did talk to me, it was short and to the point, and as little as possible was said. When she died, I remember feeling relieved that I did not have to see her any more.

My first memory of my sister is when she came to our room for a very short visit on my third birthday. She brought me yellow Playdough® and we sat on the floor and made little yellow chickens. She was beautiful, smart, and nice, and I knew I loved her. I could not understand why she did not live with us. I wanted her to so badly. I thought if she lived with us, my father would not do the things he was doing to me. Of course, that is utter nonsense, but what did I know? I was three years old.

In 1950, my grandparents were allowed to leave East Germany and join us. The name of our little town was Marienfeld. About fifty families lived there. It was a picturesque little town. My grandparents lived about a mile out of town in a four-plex apartment building which was owned by the family.

My sister contracted Scarlet Fever. We had been together for a few days at my grandparents' home when they discovered the Scarlet Fever. They came to take her to the hospital and decided since I had been exposed, they would take me as well. When you take a well child and put her into a hospital ward with ten to fifteen sick kids, there are going to be a few problems. This hospital room was wonderful. It had huge windows and the inside ledges of these windows were probably eighteen inches deep, certainly deep enough for one very small girl to stand on and play theater. The beds made wonderful trampolines. What fun it was to jump from bed to bed. Unfortunately, some of the nurses did not understand, nor did they have the slightest sense of humor . . . except one. She winked at me and did special things for me. She sat and read books to me and also sneaked in treats for me. After I had been there about a week, one of the night nurses had had enough of my antics and decided I needed to be put into bed restraints at night. (Now, you do not put sexually abused children into any kind of restraint as it is a total threat to their safety.) I screamed and carried on to the point of exhaustion. When I could not cry anymore, I pretended to be asleep. I am sure I did drift off to sleep now and again but each sound would wake and startle me. The fear that someone would come and do something hurtful to me was overwhelming. In the mornings, when the day nurse came in for her shift, she did not bother to untie the restraints–instead, she cut them to pieces. One morning, after a week of this, she came in early and yelled at the nurse who restrained me. After that morning, I was not tied down again.

My sister was very ill with the fever. I don't remember getting terribly sick. All I know is that eight weeks in a hospital room was torture in one way for me but a big relief in another. I was away from home–away from my father's abuse. My only mission in life was finding a way to stay away from him. Fear was all I felt for him. If he was not beating me, then he was lying about me, which was all a part of his setup. He had to make sure that no one would ever believe me in case I told anyone what he was doing to me. He needed to make me out to be a liar so he would be believed when he denied doing those awful things. His accusations that I said things I did not say and did things I did not do seemed to escalate with each passing day.

5 My Grandparents

My grandparents' apartment was very small. There was room enough for the two of them but any more than that was overcrowded. The bathroom facility was a double hole outhouse. There was a room built onto the apartment house which was used in a combination of ways. It was for bathing, it held kindling wood, and there was a coal cellar with a metal door with a lock on it that was like the door of a jail. There was a wonderful little creek which ran right behind the apartment building. I called my grandfather Opa, and my grandmother, Oma. That was common usage in Germany.

An aunt also lived in one of the upstairs apartments. The

other main floor apartment had been rented by what my father called "filthy foreigners." I was not allowed to play with their children. I did, however, whenever he was not around. One day I went inside to play with their little girl. The mother sat us all down to read us a story. I will never forget that story! It was all about the Devil and all that he would do to bad children. It scared me to death, and I never again went into their house.

My grandfather was the most wonderful man I knew. He was loving, compassionate, funny, patient, and very easy going. Not much could shake him up. If he worried about anything or pondered about a problem, he sat outside and whittled wood into kindling pieces. He took life on life's terms, and made the very best of every situation. Afternoon coffee time was a very special time for me with my Opa. We sat down together for coffee, tea, and some small thing to eat, but most of all for conversation. My grandfather's favorite pastime was talking. He had wonderful stories and great ways of telling them. The most fascinating thing about coffee time for me was watching my grandfather prepare his coffee. Oma would pour him a cup of coffee to which he added a teaspoon of sugar. Then the ritual began. He gently stirred and stirred, talking all the while. About the time you figured he was going to take a drink, he would take another teaspoon of sugar, add it to his coffee, stir and stir, and continue to talk. Once in a while, he actually took a sip of his coffee.

My grandfather did not allow food to be thrown away. Whatever was left over each day would be put into the pantry and he would eat it the next day. I remember seeing him take dried out pieces of bread so hard they were like rocks and dunk them in coffee or soup for softening so he could eat them. He never forgot all the times he and the family had gone hungry in the past. Throwing food away was not an acceptable thing to do because of his experiences.

Opa had a garden every summer. The children knew it was virtually a sacred place and did not dare to go into it without permission. He allowed me to come with him into his garden and taught me many things about gardening. He used to tell me that as long as one could grow a garden, one would not go hungry, but it needed to be tended with loving care and respect.

Opa did not believe in going to church but he lived by God's laws. I do not know what had soured him on going to church. He believed that one did not need to go into a building in order to worship God. I believe he worshipped God on the daily walks he took through the woods. Opa and I took many walks together and he talked to me about whatever I wanted to know. He listened to what I thought about things and when I was with him, I felt valuable, important, intelligent, and loved. He did not tell me what to do about anything, but gave me options about what to do in any situation. Whenever someone scolded me, Opa would say, "You just don't understand her." When I was at Opa's, I had the freedom to play and have fun. I loved the creek behind his house. The water was as clear as glass. You could see each small pebble on the bottom. In the summer we were allowed to swim in it. This creek wound its way through the fields and then through town. I caught tadpoles and let them wiggle in my hands. There were tiny fish that swam all around. Flowers grew up along the side of the banks. Where there were no rocks along the bottom, there was wonderful sand that felt good to walk on. In one place, the creek water seemed to be playing with the rocks as it gushed over them. In other places, it ran quietly and smoothly. The sound of the water was very soothing to me.

I saw Opa angry only once. My father had come to his house early one afternoon. During his visit, my father accused me of lying to him about something and he locked me in the coal cellar. When my grandfather came home in the evening, hours later, he found me scared and crying in the cellar. My father had left me there. Neither Oma nor my mother dared let me out because my father said he would come back to let me out, but by evening, he had not come back. That was the only time I ever heard my grandfather yell at anyone.

That day I almost told Opa what my father was doing to me. I thought about it and every fiber of my body wanted to scream it out. Then, almost at the same time, I thought what if he did not believe me? What if? That thought kept me from saying what I needed to say. I could not take the chance of losing the only person I believed really loved me just for who I was. Besides, it would hurt him and I did not want to hurt him. If I did tell him, would he also think I was bad like my father said I was? I could not take the risk. Shortly after, I was again at Opa's house when I was told that my father was coming to get me. I don't know whether he was coming to take me home or what. All I know is that I was so upset, I ran toward the woods. I thought if I could just make it to the forest, he could not find me because I could hide there. He came after me with his bicycle and caught me. He took me by my hair and dragged me next to the bicycle until we got near enough to the house where someone could see what he was doing. Then he let go of my hair and made me run in front of the bicycle until we got to my grandparents' yard.

My grandmother was a mystery to me. I know that she took care of me a lot, but I clearly remember her only a few times. Once was when she allowed me to make tomato salad. I must have been six years old. She gave me all the fixings to make it. She put a table outside the apartment and let me do it all by myself. Since every morsel of food was sacred to all of us, allowing me to do this was amazing. When I was done, she came and tasted it and raved about how good it was. When my mother came home, she also thought it was excellent and so did my aunt. I had such fun and was so proud of my accomplishment. My father came by a while later and when he tasted it, he said nothing about whether he liked it or not. He did say, however, he was sure I must have made a terrible mess. Of course that spoiled all my pride and excitement.

Oma did not seem like a happy person. She did her duties as a housewife and she took care of me when needed. I don't remember her laughing, or hugging or touching me or anyone else. I just remember she was there, always present, always doing something, stern of face and regimented in action. She would scold me by shaking her finger at me. I know she made a great difference in my life because she took care of me as much as she did. I wish I could better remember the time I spent with her.

There were times all of our relatives would come to Opa and Oma's for a get-together. There was a lot of laughing and singing during those times. Even my father would laugh, which was very unusual to hear. I would sing my heart out only to have my father stare at me to quit. Even so, they were still some of the best times I can remember.

6 Field of Daisies

Just a little way from Opa's apartment, next to another creek, there was a wild daisy field. The daisies were very tall and the flower heads seemed gigantic to me. My sister would come and sometimes go into the field with me. One day we sat in there and she taught me how to make a daisy wreath for my head. When I was upset, scared, or just wanted to be alone, I went deep inside the field by myself and sat there for hours making wreaths. In the winters, of course, I could not physically go to hide in the field. However, I soon managed to go to the field mentally, no matter where I was or what season it was. I was somehow able to mentally put myself there whenever I was beaten or molested.

While I was in that state of disassociation, I could watch, to a very short extent, what was being done to that little girl's body (my body). I felt totally separated from it. I wanted to take her with me to protect her but I knew I could not because if I did, the pain would be there. I could not survive the pain. So, in my mind, I went to the field alone and left her behind. My field was full of magic and wonder. In it, I had a pure white horse, faster than the wind. He took me through the fields and meadows into a beautiful valley where we rested and I played with all the wild animals. I used this method of escape for years to come.

7 Time for School

The first day of school in Germany is a very festive occasion. There is a tradition that each child is given a fancy cone-shaped bag full of supplies, candy, and a stuffed mouse on the first day. Now, it was imperative that the bag contain a mouse. My understanding was that the mouse would help one in one's studies. My mother had registered me and the closer it got to that first day, the more excited I became. Then a couple of days before I was to go, I heard my mother and father arguing. He said I was not going to get a bag of goodies because I did not deserve it. I was devastated. It would let everyone know just how bad I was. I no longer wanted to go to school. I ran to my daisy field and cried so hard it felt like I had nothing left inside of me–as if I were a mere shell. My sister found me there. We talked and she said I should not worry because it was not up to my father alone whether or not I would receive a bag. Now I felt something I had not felt before. Hope and doubt were all mixed up together. Hope, that I would get a bag and not have to be humiliated and ashamed; and doubt, because I could not believe that anyone could be more powerful than my father, but I certainly wanted to believe that he was not all that powerful.

I went to my first day of school with my heart pounding in my throat. My sister and mother were with me. On the way, I saw some children carrying their bags. By the time we reached the school, tears were welling up inside of me. I knew I would not get a bag and all the other children would shun me because of it. Just before we were at the front door of the school, my mother asked me to wait a minute before I went in. She went somewhere for just a minute and came back with the most beautiful treat bag. It was nicer than anyone else's. I was so relieved I cried and laughed all at the same time. I guessed I was not as bad as my father said I was after all.

From my grandparents' home to school, there were four small wooden bridges which we had to cross. More times than not, on the way to or from school, I fell into the creek from one of those bridges. My coming to school wet, or coming home wet, got to be totally frustrating for the adults in my life and also for me. I even tried to crawl across these bridges on all fours so I would not fall in. I became very fearful of crossing them because I would get punished and ridiculed when I fell in.

One day my mother sent my sister to town to get sugar and butter. My sister talked me into coming with her. We would take her bike and I could ride on the back while she steered it. That way it would not be possible for me to fall into the creek. I agreed to go, feeling very apprehensive and not fully believing her. On the way to town, everything was fine and I felt great relief. On the way home with the precious cargo we were carrying, the bike slipped sideways on one of the bridges and we both went flying. The sugar and butter ended up in the creek along with me. I hit my head on a rock but other than being shaken and fearing punishment, I was okay. My sister was stunned. She looked at me as if she thought I had made this happen. The thing I remember most clearly about this is how afraid we both were of getting punished. Things were very tough financially. When my sister explained what had happened, everyone looked at me quite strangely. It also was the first time my mother seemed to really believe that falling into the creek was not something I was doing on purpose. After this incident, the family and neighbors decided that we should all take an alternate route to school. The way was a bit longer, but there was only one main bridge to cross and it had high side rails on it. Instead of walking to school alone the long way around, some of the children decided to walk with me. It was the first time I felt important to the other children. There seemed to be no reasonable or logical explanation for my falling off the bridges all the time. The explanation came much later in my life.

I do not remember going to school between first grade and the age of eight. My mother told me that I did not finish first grade. The problem was not intelligence. In fact, I always got perfect papers on everything. One day I came home with an answer wrong and my mother asked why I had it wrong since I knew the right answer. I told her I wanted to be like everyone else! My health was so bad, however, that the school decided it was not in my best interest to stay in school at the time. I remember studying at home after that.

I was taken to a doctor because there was something wrong with the way my rib cage was growing. It was growing in on itself in the center of my chest and where the bones met, they protruded outward.

They put me on my stomach on a surgical table and formed a cast of my back. I was told I had to be strapped into this cast every night and that is how I needed to sleep. I had to do this for a long time until my bones straightened out. Panic set in. The thought of not even having the chance to protect myself from my father frightened me to the point of hysteria.

I was moved to my grandparents' house and stayed there during the time I had to be in the cast. They took care of me day and night. I loved being there and felt safe and protected.

I had the cast on for close to a year. During that time I had to go back to the doctor periodically to get checked. When I went, they put me into a thing which looked like a tunnel. It fit over my body from my neck to my knees. It had a light inside of it so it warmed my whole body. After I was done with that, I got the most wonderful back massages.

During that summer, I remember walking home to Opa's house one day. I don't know where I was coming from, but I do know I was terribly upset about something. I picked up a piece of brick I found on my way and started to throw it into the air. As I walked along doing this, I wondered what it would feel like to die. I thought if I threw this piece of brick high enough into the air and let it fall on my head, perhaps it would kill me. I hoped that it would. I threw it as high as I could several times and tried to duck under it as it came down. I missed each time! I walked a while longer holding the brick, and decided to try once more. This time the brick landed straight on top of my head. I did not feel any pain, but I did feel something trickle down my head and I put my hand there. I looked at my hand, and it was covered with blood. That scared me, so I ran as fast as I could to my grandparents' house, crying all the way. My mother was there and I told her what I had done. She just shook her head at me and patched me up.

Behind the apartment building and right across the creek was a farm, and a little girl lived there. I was allowed to play with her. I don't know if she belonged there or if she was just visiting for one summer. She and I had a wonderful time together. We were playing out in the courtyard one day when she ran into the house for something. All of a sudden, we heard a terrible scream come from inside the house. The adults ran inside. The woman came running back outside a second later and yelled for my mother to come over quickly. My little friend had pulled a boiling pot of potatoes on top of herself and it went all down her back and legs. My mother ran over to try to help. They poured vinegar over the burn right away and then took some kind of grease and gently covered the burn. She had blisters all over her back and down her legs by this time. She sat on a wooden rocking horse and rocked and cried. Someone came to get her and took her to the hospital or to a doctor. I never saw her again and no one ever told me if she was all right.

It has taken me years to remember good times with certain people in my childhood and remembering those times seems to be an ongoing process for me. Perhaps it is because there were very few genuinely good times. Somehow, whenever I felt happiness, joy, or excitement about something, my father was there to spoil it by either verbally putting me down, shaming me for laughing too loud, or punishing me afterwards. So feeling joy about anything was real risky because I would pay for feeling it. When he was not around, I could be happy without fear of punishment, but the fear was there nonetheless.

I believed my sister cared deeply for me and I loved her as much as I was angry with her. I wanted her to save me, but each time I saw her, she would have to leave again. I felt abandoned by her. Yet I loved every moment I could spend with her. She told me not too long ago that when she baby-sat me, I would hit her and be very mean to her. She said once I took after her with a broom. I don't recall any times with her except good times, however. I know that there are still many things locked away in my memory and perhaps some of them are better locked away forever.

I have very few memories of my mother during my early years. Besides the times I have already told you about, I remember when she and I would go into the forest to pick mushrooms and berries. She took care of me the many times I had the measles, and she was there when I had the mumps, and when I had my tonsils taken out. Those memories are not sharp and clear; they seem distant and vague. I cannot remember her physical touch, nor do I remember an emotional closeness to her at this time. One of the reasons I don't remember her much is because she worked as many hours as she could to help out financially.

8 The City

We moved to the city, Bottrop-Boy, when I was eight. It meant being away from the safety of my grandparents. The only reason I did not panic about the move was because I was told my sister would be going with us and living with us. Somehow that made it seem not quite so risky.

Bottrop was a coal mining town. My father worked in the mines. Every day, within minutes of when we went outside, our eyes burned because the air was laden with coal dust. Our tears flowed involuntarily to clean out our eyes. After about half an hour, our eyes would get used to it and stop burning. My mother had to dust the furniture and clean the floors daily just to keep the coal dust under control inside our apartment. Every day the rags she used were black when she finished.

We had moved into a seemingly huge apartment complex. It was the first real home I remember living in with my parents since my third birthday. I do not remember living with them after I was three years old. I did live with them, but all I remember is being with my grandparents.

Now we had our own place with a living room, kitchen, and indoor bathroom.

I remember my sister living with us only when she began to work at a store. I did not see her very much because she was working ten to twelve hours a day. At that time, children in Germany completed their education in the eighth grade which was equivalent to a high school education in the United States. She was gone before I had to get up for school and came home late afternoon or early evening. She was now in the bedroom with me at night and I was glad of that.

My parents did not fight like they used to. My mother was home all the time now. I felt safer there for some reason but I don't exactly know why. I even seemed to be a little more comfortable with my father. He apparently did not feel he had the opportunity to continue his sexual abuse because it stopped while we lived there. He did continue the psychological abuse which got more intense as we lived there longer.

For example, my father had me polish his shoes for him. One particular day, I spent what seemed like hours polishing them, and when I was done, I proudly brought them to him. He looked at them, and then at me, and said, "I told you to polish them." I said I had and he called me a liar, slapped me, and told me to go polish them. I was devastated. I had worked so hard on them and was so sure he would be pleased with me for once. His verbal abuse toward me was horrendous. He did not smile at me or praise me for anything, and never touched me other than to smack me. He let me know that I could do nothing right, that I was stupid, that I was no good, and that I certainly would not amount to anything. I heard these things from him time and time again. When he was not saying these things, he would look at me in a way that told me I disgusted him just by being alive.

I developed a terrible facial tic. It started shortly after we moved to the city. There seemed to be no good explanation for it, but then, no one asked me why my face twitched and contorted. No one noticed that whenever my father was around me, it got worse. Somehow it got blamed on the poor nutrition I had while growing up.

I was allowed to play with some of the kids in the complex but not all of them because, according to my father, there were some pretty undesirable people living there. The ones I were allowed to play with could actually come into our apartment now and again, and I could go into theirs. That was a big deal to me because I had not been allowed to go into anyone's home without my parents before.

Two blocks away, a street was blocked off to traffic and used by the children for roller skating. I went down there and watched the kids, wishing I could skate. I talked to a little girl who was skating one day. She asked me why I didn't skate, too. I told her it was because I did not have skates. She left and in a few minutes she came back with a pair of skates. She said they were her old ones and they did not fit her anymore. She said I could have them. I knew my father would not allow me to take them from her, so I told her I would just use them when I could come and skate. She stayed with me and attempted to teach me how to skate. I went back every day I could to skate with her.

My skating friend's name was Monika. Both of her parents were deaf. When I first met them, I did not know how to act around them. Monika and her parents were kind and wonderful people, and it took no time at all before I was completely at ease with them. Monika ended up being my very special friend.

I was given a pair of roller skates. Every chance I had, and every minute I could, I skated with my friends. To zoom along that street gave me a feeling of freedom. I became very good at skating and did things on my roller skates that one would normally see done only on ice skates. I took great pride in how I risked learning new stunts and turns.

School in the city was just about as bad as being at home with my father. My class had sixty children and one teacher. It was regimented and totally authoritarian. We had to sit just so in our seats. If we slouched, we felt a stick crash across our backs. If we were asked a question and gave a wrong answer, we had to stand by our desk, hold out a hand and get smacked with a stick across our hand. With any kind of misbehavior, we ended up over the teacher's knees and got a whipping with the stick in front of the whole class.

Disrespect toward an adult from a child was a reason for capital punishment. My friends and I were playing outside one evening when my teacher walked by. He looked at me and I was startled, so I ran off. The proper thing for me to do was to stop doing whatever I was doing, acknowledge him, and curtsey to show my respect. The next day, my teacher talked to my father about my disrespect and, of course, my father beat me. I was also not allowed to skate for a long time, nor could I play outside with my friends.

My uncle and his wife lived close enough to us so we could see them quite often. My uncle was a happy-go-lucky sort of person and I liked being around him. Even my father was different when we all got together. He would actually smile, laugh, and sing along with everyone.

Right from the beginning of our time in the city, my mother's behavior toward my father changed. She became more assertive toward him. She stuck up for me when she thought he was out of line. She only succeeded to a limited degree, but at least I saw her trying to protect and help me.

One day, when she and my father were arguing about me, I heard her threaten to tell the neighbors how unreasonable and mean he was. He calmed right down and quit arguing with her. A light went on in my mind—my father was afraid to have anyone outside of the immediate family know how he treated his family. Until then I could not figure out why he was so different in his behavior whenever outsiders, including relatives, were around us nor how other people seemed to like and respect him. Now I knew. He was a totally different person, personality- and behavior-wise, outside of his home. He worked very hard to be liked and respected in the community. He knew all the right behaviors to accomplish that but when he closed the door behind him in his own home, he turned mean. I have often wondered which one of his personalities was the real soul of this man.

I began to trust my mother and rely on her to protect me when my father would try to hurt me. From this point on, my mother is no longer just a vague memory to me. Now Mom and I would go to the market together, and go on walks, and sing together, and make lunches together. She came to watch me roller skate several times. These things may seem dull and mundane, but I celebrated each moment I could spend with my mother. Because of her assertiveness with my father, I was able to go to a Spring Party that all the children in the building went to. The celebration was called Kinderfest and was celebrated each year. It was a day set aside for children and was celebrated with parades and carnivals. My mother took my sister and me to the carnival that year. There were swings which were good-sized boats. People sat in them and manually pumped until they were swinging as high as they wanted to go. After a certain amount of time, the attendant put the brakes on underneath the boat to slow it down until it stopped. My sister and I had a wonderful time riding in these.

My mother saw to it that I had a birthday party on my tenth birthday. She had to talk, fight, and insist long and hard before my father allowed this. He wanted me to have none of these things.

My mother also took me to see my first movie. It starred Shirley Temple in a story about her parents' divorce and how she got them to reconcile their marriage. It was a tear-jerker. There could not have been a dry eye in the theater at the end of that movie. I did not allow myself to cry very often when I was a child. You see, I could not be weak or seem weak to my father, because then he would know he had gotten the best of me. After this movie, I could not stop crying for a long while. I cried first because of the story, then I cried for myself because I wanted a father like the one in that movie. I wanted the love from him I saw in that story and I knew that I could not have it. That was the first time I consciously felt sorry for myself.

The first time I remember my mother laughing was when just she and I were alone in our apartment. We were singing and we both messed up the song and she found it funny.

I vividly recall only one Christmas and that was when I was nine. My mother and father had my sister and me go into our room. We were told to not come out until we heard them sing a certain Christmas song. While we were in our room, my sister brought out two beautiful cup and saucer sets. We were to give these to my mother when we went into the living room. We would carry them in to her. I have no idea if we had anything for my father. If we did, I don't remember what it was. Finally, after a long time, we heard them sing. We very carefully walked into the living room. All the lights were out and yet there was a light coming from in there. As we walked in, I saw the most beautiful Christmas tree full of burning candles and underneath it were presents. It was the most glorious thing I had ever seen! We received a plate full of good things to eat–a big bar of chocolate, fruit, a can of sweetened condensed milk, apple juice, and small pieces of candy. That is the only Christmas I remember celebrating with my parents in Germany and it would be the only Christmas not spoiled for me by my father.

There were a few other holidays when we got together with all the relatives. That was great fun because of all the laughing and singing. My grandfather played several instruments but the one I remember him playing most was the harmonica. We sang along as he played it. During these festive occasions, the children had to be extra specially good because if they were not, they would get put to bed. Since I grew up in the era where children were to be seen and not heard, I had a very difficult time. I wanted to join in and the louder my grandfather would sing, the louder I sang with him, until my father ordered me to bed because I had gotten too loud. There were a few times when everyone told him to leave me alone and let me stay. Of course that was wonderful, but the fun was already over for me because my father had once again managed to shame me. I remember feelings of humiliation, shame, hurt, disappointment, and fear as I grew up. There was an unwritten rule that children had no right to ever be angry. Certainly, a child had no right or reason to be angry with his or her parents, so I did not consciously feel anger.

9 The Dream

Back when my father was a POW in Italy, he fell in love with the United States as seen through the eyes of the American major for whom he drove. He was determined to emigrate to America. He applied for the emigration permission sometime after his release from prison camp.

In the fall of 1955, my parents got up one morning and each of them had had the same dream the previous night–a letter was going to be in the mail from America. The following day, the letter arrived. Someone had accepted sponsorship of our family; we could live in the U.S.! My parents started to make arrangements right away.

We were to leave Germany by ship at the end of January or beginning of February, 1956. The next few months were spent in preparation for this trip. I watched as it was decided what we could take and what we would sell. There were also things we would have to give away, like the precious few toys I had. I had a teddy bear, a doll, roller skates, and a ball which I had received on my tenth birthday. Other than that, I don't remember any toys I may have had. I gave the teddy bear to a little boy in the next building because he had less than I did. I did not want to leave my doll, so I was told I could have it sent over by my aunt. The rest I had to give away. I gave my roller skates to Monika and told her to find someone who could use them.

We had to get physicals and immunizations. After my physical, the doctors told my parents that I had to gain some weight or they were afraid I would not survive the boat trip. I was ten years old and weighed forty-five pounds. They said I had to gain five pounds, minimum, in order for them to okay my going. They suggested sending me to a children's home which dealt with children's health problems, including low weight. If I did not gain the weight I needed to, my parents could not leave Germany and that would have been the end of my father's dream. The name of the home I went to was Dünenrose. It was a private children's home, but that did not matter since everything was paid for by the German government. Germany had socialized medicine at that time. I was to be there for up to six weeks to gain the weight I needed. I was scared to go. I would be with complete strangers and as I had no reason to trust people I knew, what would happen to me with strangers? My mother talked with me about going and what fun it would be because they did a lot of wonderful things with the children such as boat rides and taking trips to parks. We went for a pre-enrollment visit and I liked the woman we talked to. No matter what I thought, I knew I had no choice in the matter, I had to go. All I remember of my time in that home was being forced to eat more than my stomach could possibly hold and having to run to the bathroom after each meal to throw up. My other memory of that place is being locked up in a bathroom to sleep all night. I had been giggling after going to bed that night and got everyone else giggling. The nurses were angry with me because we were all supposed to be quiet and go to sleep, so I ended up locked in the bathroom for the night. When the time came to go home, I had gained the five pounds I needed to gain. It was just enough and they allowed my family to leave Germany.

Chapter 2 - Going to America

10 Ocean Voyage

With all the excitement in preparation for our trip, my parents were getting along quite well. My father was also treating me better. He would talk to me, and, for the first time, I saw him smile directly at me. I was not sure whether to trust the change. Our relatives threw a good-bye party for us on the New Year's Eve before we were to leave. They had fireworks, wonderful food, and lots of singing. My father verbally put me down only once that whole day. That night, I was allowed to drink a glass of champagne with the adults. From that point on, I remember nothing of that night. The next day, my father proceeded to tell me all the things I had done and how angry he was with me. I did not believe him. He lied about me all the time, and I did not remember doing any of the things he said I had done. Later, I asked my mother, sister, and aunt about what he said. They confirmed that what he told me was true. I could not understand why I did not remember, and believed something was happening to me which was really scary. From that day on, when my father accused me of doing or saying anything which I did not remember, I could not be sure that he was not right. I started to question my sanity and my concept of reality.

My school had a farewell party for me. This was highly unusual because school was serious business and not a place to have fun. The party was a total and pleasant surprise. I felt terribly important and sad. That day, it finally hit me that this was all real. We were leaving Germany. All of a sudden, I was scared. I realized I would not see my grandfather again.

Fear gripped me so intensely I could hardly move.

The day we took the train to the port of departure, my grandparents came to see us off and to say good-bye. I clung to Opa so hard that they had to pull me away from him to put me on the train. I did not want to go. I wanted to stay with Opa. We took the train to some buildings which had been used as barracks for the soldiers during the war. We stayed there for a few days while we went through more physicals, shots, and all the paperwork we had to take along.

The day finally came when we were to board the ship. It was an ugly cargo ship which had been used in World War II. The hull of the ship was made into sleeping quarters. It had two big rooms separated in the middle by a line of bathrooms. On either side of the bathrooms were army cots stacked four and five high, crammed together in rows. The men were to sleep on one side of the bathrooms and the women and children on the other. It was drab, dull, and smelly. They also had one area set up with tables, much like long picnic tables, where we all went to eat. There must have been between five hundred to a thousand people on the ship. It seemed more like ten thousand to me. After everyone had boarded, found their cots, and stored their luggage wherever they could–preferably under their cots–we were given instructions about the trip. There were certain times we could be on deck. We were shown how to use life jackets and how to get the lifeboats down. We were all given paper sacks which we needed to carry with us at all times in case we became seasick.

My bunk was the second from the bottom in a stack of four. An old woman in her eighties was on the bunk below me. She was going to America to be with her daughter who had emigrated a few years earlier. She was a soft-spoken, gentle person. I talked to her whenever I could. During the trip, she got terribly seasick and after a few days at sea, she could no longer get out of bed other than to go to the bathroom. Someone brought her food at mealtimes, but she could eat little.

The first few days at sea were not too bad for me. We were allowed on deck much of the time because the weather was nice. It felt good to be in the fresh air. The air in the hull was stale and stagnant. A few people were already getting seasick and it did not smell very good down there. The food was awful (and that is being said by someone who eats just about anything). If the rolling of the sea did not make one sick, the food did. I had to eat what I could to keep my strength up.

As each day passed, the sea became rougher. More and more people were getting seasick, and as the sea got more turbulent, we were allowed less and less time on deck. The stench got so bad below that one would get sick from it. By the time we had been at sea for a week, it felt like we had been underway for a month and it would never end. I was beginning to doubt that we would ever see land again.

I was allowed on deck one day when the sea was very rough. I had to hang on to a post in order to not get thrown around by the motion of the ship. I looked at the water and it was above me. The sea was so rough that the ship would go down into what seemed like a deep crater. As it went down into this crater, the water came up all around the ship until it looked like the water would swallow it up. The ship would somehow come out of this crater of water only to go deep into another one. We were hit by a major storm that night. When we got up in the morning, everyone's belongings were on one side of the ship. We all had to find our things and retrieve them. A number of people died that night, including the woman who bunked below me. The storm had also thrown us off course, so we were at sea a couple of extra days. By this time, I figured we would all die in that awful ship and they were just putting off the inevitable.

One day, two weeks after leaving Germany, an announcement came over the loudspeaker that if we wanted our first glimpse of the Statue of Liberty, we should get on deck. As we looked out onto the horizon, there was the slightest protrusion which seemed to rise out of the water. The longer we looked, the bigger it got, until finally we could see the head of the statue. The whole ship seemed to explode into cheers. People were crying and laughing all at the same time. Thank God we had made it! We pulled into the New York harbor on February 14, 1956. It was a month before my eleventh birthday.

We gathered our things together. All we had were a few suitcases. We were ready to get off that ship, the sooner the better, and we hoped to never see it or anything like it again.

We were checked through Ellis Island and stood in long lines as everyone's papers and luggage was thoroughly checked. Some people who had gone through ahead of us had been taken aside and were crying. Their papers apparently were not in order and it was not sure if they could stay. I was scared they would not let us stay and I felt I would rather die than to have to get back on that ship to go back. In what seemed like hours, we were checked through and told we could go.

We had to take a train to Minnesota. It was a beautiful ride. The scenery was gorgeous and there was so much to see. We went the northern route via Chicago and then to

Mankato, Minnesota. Someone in Germany said they heard America had streets paved with gold. I did not see any of that, but the vastness and beauty of this country seemed just as good as gold to me. When we came close to the Mankato station, we were all tired, excited and apprehensive. We did not know the people who sponsored us or how they lived. Where would we live? How could I communicate? I did not speak English. How could I go to school when I didn't speak the language? Would anyone like me? A hundred different thoughts kept bombarding my mind until the train came to a stop. We got off the train and collected our luggage. There they were, our sponsors, Al and Ina. Their faces were lit up with smiles and I could feel their excitement. They grabbed and hugged my sister and me. I quickly fell in love with them. (In Germany, people rarely hug or show such blatant emotion. Even within a family unit, you shake hands, you don't hug.) We got into Al and Ina's car. What a wonderful ride that was! I had never been in a car before! On the ride to our destination, Ina talked and talked to my father and he translated to us when necessary. She smiled constantly, put her arm around me, and hugged me time and time again. I loved every moment of all this attention. Al reminded me of Opa. He seemed to be laid back, patient, and he smiled a lot like Opa. He had the special twinkle in his eyes I had seen in Opa's eyes so many times. I felt very comfortable around him. As we kept on driving, it seemed like we were heading for the wilderness. I had never seen so much snow, and the open land seemed to go on forever. Everything was so massive. Even the farm houses we saw were huge and they were made of wood, not brick. In Germany, every building I had ever seen was brick. Everything was different from what I had known. When we pulled up to Al and Ina's home, our long journey was over at last and our new life was about to begin.

11 A New Culture

Our sponsors owned the Gamble-Skogmo store in the little town where they lived. Al ran the parts department, where he sold everything from nuts to bolts. His store catered to the farmers since it was a small farming community. Ina was responsible for the rest of the store, which contained just about everything one would ever need for a household, other than furniture. Attached to the rear of the store was their home. It was a cute little apartment which consisted of a kitchen, living room, one bedroom, and a bathroom. We were used to small places, so we did not give a second thought to the size of their place. They had a pullout couch, which either my sister and I, or my mother and father would sleep on. They set up a couple of roll-away beds in the back of the store for whoever wanted to sleep out there. My mother and father were the ones to end up sleeping out in the store.

Our sponsors had a television! I had not seen such a thing before and I was fascinated with it. Ina would turn it on for me and let me watch cartoons. Those cartoons, as much as anything else, helped me learn English very quickly because I wanted to understand what was being said. Also, I had never seen, nor talked on, a telephone! There were so many things I had not experienced before, and they seemed to come all at once.

The second Sunday after we arrived, we went to church with Al and Ina. It was a little Lutheran church in town—the same one through which they had sponsored us. Everyone stared at us the whole time. I felt like I was something put on display for everyone. Our sponsors went to church every Sunday. They had done this all of their lives, so it was a given fact that we would go to church with them. We rarely went to church while we lived in Germany. I do recall being there twice. The first time, I was told to dip my fingers into the water that was at the entrance of the church and cross myself before we went in to sit down. The second time, I was dressed all in white with a garland on my head. We proceeded to go outside and walked down the streets behind the priest. He had Holy Water which he sprinkled as we walked and sang. There were others carrying huge banners of some sort. It was apparently a very special occasion. (I presume it was my first communion.)

The first few weeks we were in our new home, Ina had me come out into the store to meet the children that came to see me. I would say hello, shake their hand, and high-tail it back to the apartment or I would start running around in the store trying to hide. That was how Ina and I got started playing hide and seek. It seemed she could turn any uncomfortable situation for me into a positive and fun time. Al would just giggle about all of my antics. Whenever my father tried to scold me about anything, Ina grabbed me, hugged me, and told him I was okay. In this situation, my father had no control and I knew it. I milked it for all it was worth.

I was fascinated with the typewriter and adding machine in Al's office. He let me stay there at night after the store closed and pound away on them to my heart's content.

Al hired my father to work in the repair shop in his garage. They fixed small engines such as lawn mowers. My father was not a nice person when it came to the relationship with his family, but he was, and always had been, a hard worker. He was not fussy about the kind of work he did as long as he could provide for his family. He worked very hard and took any job he could get so that we would have the money to get out on our own.

My sister and I were enrolled in school, which was a Godsend to my sister. She loved to learn and it also meant she did not have to work again for the next couple of years. Being able to go back to school was like a dream come true for her after working as hard as she had at her job in Germany. I, on the other hand, was not real excited about going back to school. I figured it was like the school I had left and certainly not something to look forward to.

School was a small country school where each teacher had two classes to teach because the class sizes were so small. I was put into the fourth grade instead of fifth where I belonged. The authorities felt I needed some extra time to adjust and learn English. The first few days, I did nothing except disrupt the classes. I sat in my chair and whenever someone would look at me, I made funny faces at them. I constantly had the classes laughing. I could not believe I was not being punished or hit for my behavior.

My teacher assigned a student to help teach me English. At the end of each day, the teacher pointed to the things for which I was to have learned the words, and I would tell her what they were. She was very patient and had a lot of praise for me every day. This certainly was different from my school in Germany. One day, the girl she assigned to me taught me nothing but swear words all day long. The kids all thought this was hilarious. Needless to say, this student was not assigned to teach me English again, but she did become my best friend, which lasted long past high school.

By summer, my father had earned enough money so we could rent our own place. The whole town came to our aid. Furniture and everything we needed to set up housekeeping was either donated to us or sold to us for little or nothing. We rented a small house in town. We moved out of our sponsor's home and began what was to be our new life. By this time, I had also learned enough English to go out by myself, play with friends I had made, and even go to their homes when invited. There was so much to explore and I was given more freedom than I had ever known.

12 A Hamlet

The town we lived in was, and is today, a small rural community. To date there are only three hundred people who live there. Everyone knew everyone else. If you did any mischief, the whole town knew about it the very next day. It actually helped to keep everyone, especially the children, pretty much in line with the social ethics and norms of the community. People were friendly and helped each other out. It reminded me of a little hamlet in a book I had read.

There was a marsh on the outskirts of town. Some of the kids and I went there to catch frogs and turtles. I brought home a good size turtle and decided to make a pet out of it. I did not know that turtles make a terrible racket when they are unhappy. After a couple of nights of loud cricket-type sounds all night long from the basement where I had made a bed for him, we decided to let him go back to the marsh.

I had quite a few friends I regularly played with. A couple of them were sisters and they were the daughters of an assistant pastor in town. I had been at their home several times to play and had a great time. One particular day when I went over there to play, one of the girls gave me a fifty-cent piece. She said it was hers and she wanted me to have it. I did not want to take it because I knew my parents would not approve of such a thing, but my friend insisted and said it was a gift from her to me. When I went home, I did not tell my mother about it because I knew she would not let me keep it. I hid it and spent it the next day. About a week later, my mother received a call from this girl's parents and they said I had stolen a fifty-cent piece from them. I said I had not, and that their daughter had given it to me. Their daughter denied ever seeing the coin. Of course my mother wanted to believe me, but how could she? After all, my father had made me out to be a liar for years. Now all she wanted me to do was to admit that I had taken the coin so I could apologize and pay it back. For days, I kept insisting I was innocent. Then my mother asked my sister to take me for a walk to talk to me about it. I admired my sister so much, and she had never lied to me or hurt me in any way. She was like an idol to me and I trusted her. She told me that everyone believed I was guilty and it would be better and easier on me if I just admitted that I had stolen the coin. Of course, my sister said, if I really had not taken it, I should not say I had. I now knew that I was going to get punished either way. If I told my parents I had taken it, they might go easy on me, and if I kept saying I had not, they would not believe me anyway. Not only was I going to get punished for something I had not done, but I would also be disgraced in front of every person in town. To get the whole mess over with, I went home and told my mother I had stolen the coin.

I was grounded the rest of that summer. I was not allowed off our property, nor was I allowed to go anywhere without the supervision of my mother or my sister. When friends came over to play with me, they were often sent away. But the worst for me was watching my mother bake cookies and cakes, and pick vegetables out of her precious garden (which she had planted and tended with such care) to give to the family of my accuser. I would go to my room and cry each time my mother took something over there. I could see her embarrassment, and it was her way of paying back what she thought I had taken. I never spoke to that girl again, in or out of school.

About four miles west of town was a lake. It was a narrow, long lake surrounded by farms. Our sponsors had a boat there, and on weekends we went with them to the lake. My sister and I swam and sunbathed on the roof of the boat. This boat was like a miniature cruiser. It was made out of beautiful wood. The second summer here, we learned how to waterski and had a wonderful time each summer thereafter.

In the fall of 1956, I was enrolled in fifth grade. In Germany, I had already studied everything that was taught, so I had extra time to become proficient in English and so, scholastically, I breezed through the fifth grade.

My parents were able to buy their own home the following year. It was the first property they had ever owned. The house needed some work done on it to bring it up to more modern standards and my parents did the repairing as they could afford it. My mother was really innovative. She could take a wooden apple crate and make the nicest cupboard out of it. By this time, we were living the good life. We had everything we needed and I saw my mother happier than I had ever seen her.

A half of block in back of our home was a drive-in. It was where teenagers gathered at night during the summers. It served hamburgers, hot dogs, pop and snacks. My bedroom window faced the drive-in, and on summer nights, I sat by my open windows listening to the talk and laughter, wishing I could be there.

My sister and I had our own rooms in our new home. Shortly after we moved in, the sexual abuse began again when my father and I were alone in the house. After a while, however, he would even come into my room in the middle of the night when everyone was home sleeping. Now I discovered that I had lost the magic of my daisy field. I could no longer escape to it as I had been able to before. As long as I had my field to escape to, I had power. Now I felt abandoned, and I had no power left. I wanted to tell my mother what was going on, but she was happier than she had ever been and I could not spoil that for her. I wanted to tell my sister, but ever since the coin incident, I did not think she would believe me. Besides, I started to blame myself. I thought there must have been something I had done to make my father do this to me again. If I told someone outside the family, it would be my word against my father's. Who would believe me? Everyone in town thought I lied about the coin so they surely would not believe me in this.

My father was respected and well liked by the adults in town. They did not know what he was like in our home. Over the last year, he had slowly reverted back to being mean, more toward me–it seemed–than to my mother or sister. There was no reason for anyone on the outside to believe my father was capable of such a thing. What if I did go to one of my teachers whom I trusted and he or she confronted my father? What if, then, I still had to live in my home? Things would be much worse than ever. I was terrified of that. So I kept this to myself and dealt with it the best I could by just surviving it. When I got to a point where I thought I just could not go on, I went over to our sponsors' house as an escape, even if it was for just a few hours at a time. I learned that I was not punished for going there, even if I had been told not to. I guess my father was too afraid I would tell them.

Toward the end of fifth grade, I decided I did not like being so much older than my classmates. I had turned twelve that year. I wanted to skip sixth grade the following year so I could be in the grade I belonged. I talked to my teacher about it and she arranged for me to get the study material I needed to accomplish this. My sister tutored me all summer. I took all the tests and I skipped the sixth grade that fall. There were consequences to that, however. Most of the kids in seventh grade thought it was unfair, and did not want to have much to do with me. So I kept my friends in the sixth grade and they remained my friends throughout the rest of my schooling. I believe I subconsciously worked so hard to skip the sixth grade because it would mean one less year of having to live with my father. Now I would graduate a year earlier.

Shortly after succeeding in skipping a grade, my father told me that if I wanted any more clothes, I needed to learn to sew them for myself. It was meant as another form of punishment. He could not stand it when I succeeded at anything, so he would make life harder for me any way he could. This, however, turned out to be the greatest gift my father ever gave me.

My mother taught me how to sew. She was a perfectionist

in everything she did, and I learned how to sew well. I found that I had a talent for sewing and designing clothes. It was the first thing I had done which I took real pride in and even my father's criticism about my sewing could not dampen my pride or joy in doing it. I finally had something I could do to feel good about and have control over. He could not ever take that away!

I joined the 4-H Club and had to sew something and prepare a dish of food to take to the County Fair for judging. I sewed an apron and embroidered it, and I decided to make my mother's recipe of German potato salad and demonstrate how to make it. I won blue ribbons for both and felt very good about my accomplishments.

My father did not like having anyone in our home except our sponsors and a couple of German friends. I started to press my mother about being able to have my friends over after school. My mother had no problem with it, and she also let me go to my friends' homes after school. I had to make sure I was home before my father came home from work, however, so that there would not be trouble between my parents over this. That way, he did not know how often my mother let me go out to my friends' homes. When my friends came to our house, they had to make sure to leave before my father got home, but they didn't mind because all my friends were afraid of my father.

My father did not want me to stay overnight at anyone's house or have any of my friends stay at ours. He did everything he could to isolate me from everyone. However, I finagled things so that I could have one friend spend a few weekend nights at our house. I did it by asking my father for permission in front of another adult. Not wanting to look mean in front of this person, my father agreed. I did this as often as I could because when my friend was there with me, I did not have to worry about my father sexually attacking me.

It was a mystery to me why my father treated me the way he did. I began to believe there must be something terrible in me that only he could see.

I believed my sister was so much better than me because my father did not treat her the way he treated me. My parents raved about her accomplishments, but not mine. I would hear "Why can't you do what your sister does?" or "Why can't you behave the way your sister does?" or "You will never be as smart as your sister." By this time, everyone in town was commenting on how beautiful she was. She seemed to be perfect and here I was, someone who could not do anything right. It seemed the harder I tried, the more criticism I got, but there was something inside of me which did not let me give up trying, no matter how hard things got.

13 Trip Out West

The family was to take a trip out west for two weeks and I was apprehensive about it. It meant being cooped up in a car every day. We would also be tenting at night, instead of staying in motels, in order to save money. I had not tented before, so I did not realize what it was all about. I did understand that we would all sleep together in the tent which made me really nervous about the whole thing.

We did go, of course, and my sister and I tried to make the very best of it. We had learned to harmonize whenever we sang together so we used our talent and sang a lot while driving down the road. My mother and father would actually join in once in a while, which made our trip quite pleasant.

We went to the Black Hills and stopped many places to go sight seeing. I remember going into a gold mine and panning for gold. We didn't find any but it was a lot of fun. I did not enjoy camping. There were too many strange noises out there in the woods. I also did not like being cooped up so close to my father.

We went to Yellowstone National Park. The night we camped there, I slept in the car because of all the bears. There was no way I was going to sleep in that flimsy tent where the bears could get at me. My father kept a gun at his side that night.

In Montana, some of the scenery was breathtaking. I bought myself a white angel blouse in the city of Billings, and I kept that blouse for many years afterwards.

We also went to California, where we swam in the ocean! I was very grateful I had my feet on the sand instead of on a ship. San Francisco was an awesome place. I will never forget driving up and down those steep streets. It was so hilly that one would come to the bottom of a hill only to discover it was actually on the top of another hill, and on and on it would go. It reminded me of that stormy day on the ocean in our ship when the water seemed as though it would swallow the boat.

Right from the beginning of our trip, we kept getting flat tires. It seemed every time we stopped anywhere and came back to our car, we had a flat tire. It was aggravating and expensive. My parents had taken all the money they could on this trip, and did not need extra expenses. My father took it in pretty good spirits, which surprised me, and he actually joked about it toward the end of our trip. He seemed to be a different person on this trip. He was relaxed and was not as short-tempered as he often was. He acted as if he really enjoyed explaining about what we were seeing and experiencing. Some of the mountains we drove through were really scary because the roads were so narrow and winding, but they did not seem to bother my father much. We were the nervous ones, because while he was driving, he did not always have his eyes on the road as he was looking everywhere else. He didn't want to miss any of the beautiful scenery either. But, all in all, our trip was a great success and it was the only time I ever really had fun with my father!

After two weeks on the road, we were all glad to be back home. I was very hopeful because now that we had been able to have such a good time together–maybe–just maybe, it would continue at home.

14 Taking Control

I was confirmed in the spring of 1959. We all knelt down at the altar for the blessing. After we recited everything we needed to, the minister put his hand on each of our heads as he gave the blessing. When he laid his hand on my head, I felt as if a jolt of electricity went throughout my body. Then I felt a calm and peace such as I had not felt before. Tears came to my eyes and I believed that God touched me through my minister, and the peace I felt stayed with me for many weeks.

There had been a knowledge deep within me that there was a force outside of myself, a presence that somehow was with me at all times–something that cared about me. Whatever I had gone through, this presence was with me. It was a knowing deep within me that I was not ever alone. I accepted it, but did not understand it. I began to realize that the presence I felt surrounding me was the spirit of God.

Sometime around my fourteenth year, my father decided to be an over-the-road truck driver. He was gone for weeks at a time. My sister graduated from high school and found a good job in Minneapolis. Now it was just my mother and me, except when my father was home between his trips. For both my mother and me, it was wonderful to have my father gone so much.

There were a few times before my father took the job as a trucker when I was allowed to be with my friends on Saturday nights and Sunday afternoons. I, of course, did what my friends did when I was with them. In a town the size of ours where Main Street is only five blocks long, the only thing to do was to walk the streets and look for cute guys from out of town. Hopefully, they would stop and talk for a while. If they did, we cased them out and decided if it was safe to ride in their cars with them. We went in groups of three or four and thought this was totally thrilling. One night my father saw me riding in a car with boys. He cut us off and told me to get out of the car. He slapped me in front of everyone and took me home.

A guy named David lived on a farm outside of town and was a friend to all of us. David would take us anywhere we wanted to go. He was kind of cute and a lot of fun. He was also 19 years old and I fell head over heels in love with him. It became terribly important that I be able to go downtown every weekend so I could see him. The weekends I was not allowed to go were awful. I would sit in my room looking out the window, listening and watching for his car to go by, and it always did. He wrote me notes on the weekends I could not see him and gave them to my friends to give to me. I was alone with David only once. He tried to get intimate with me that evening and I told him no. He stopped and said he would not be so forward again. I was to tell him when I wanted more than a platonic relationship with him and until then, he would wait.

My parents found out I was seeing David and grounded me for six weeks during my fourteenth summer. I could not go anywhere without my mother, and only two of my friends were allowed to come to my house.

At this point in my life, I started to try to control outside situations and people around me in order to get my way. I had already learned that I could manipulate certain situations, but now I took it a step further. After a few weeks of being grounded, I had had enough. I was sitting on our porch with one of my friends and told her I was going to run away. She helped me plan where I would go and told me she would call David to let him know what I was going to do. She asked him to meet me downtown at a specific place and time. So I ran away and David was at the appointed place and time to meet me. I jumped in his car and we left town. We drove for a while and stopped on a country road to talk about what to do next. I wanted him to drive to another state and marry me so I could get out of my parents' home, but he convinced me that it was not a good idea, even though he wanted to marry me. He wanted me to finish high school and said he would wait for me no matter what. We would see each other whenever we could sneak away and be together. David talked me into going home. I called my mother at ten o'clock that evening and asked her what she would do to me if I came home. She said, "Nothing, just come home." My father was on a run out to California with his truck, so I did not have to worry about him being home. Hopefully, he would never know I had run away.

I went home. My mother and sister were there. My mother was on the phone as I walked in. She turned to me and said my father wanted to talk to me. I shook with fright as I took the phone. Even though he was in California, I trembled out of fear of him. He asked me what I thought I was doing worrying my mother like I had and what was the matter with me? Then he said I had better shape up because the next time I caused any trouble whatsoever, he was going to put me into a detention home. I felt myself boiling inside. Until this day, I had not dared to speak back to my father. When he threatened me this time, I fought back. I said to him, "You just try it and I think you know what will happen." Then I slammed the phone down. I turned around and saw frightened looks on the faces of my mother and my sister. As I turned to go upstairs to my room, my mother physically tried to stop me at the bottom of the stairs. She was asking me how I could talk to my father that way. I turned around and slapped her, then I ran upstairs to my room. I was angry at everyone in my family. They had all let me down in one way or another. I had felt sorry for my mother because I thought she had to put up with my father. I knew better now. I did not feel sorry for her any longer. I was sick of her playing my father's games and not standing up to him. It was days before my mother and I said anything to each other. I stayed in my room most of the time.

After a couple of days had passed, I felt guilty about hitting her. The day my father came home from his trip to California, I was shaking inside and out. I had no idea what he would do to me, but I envisioned all kinds of awful things.

He did absolutely nothing to me. He did not even talk to me about my running away. The next day, the only thing he said to me was that I was never to hit my mother again for any reason. They both told me that I was not to see David again and that if I did, I would be grounded until I graduated. I knew they meant it. This may seem excessive, but since my father was not physically hurting me, this was the most reasonable I had ever seen him so I agreed.

To my amazement, my father never again attempted to sexually touch me. I figured he was afraid of the threat I made to him over the phone. He could no longer be sure that I would not tell someone what he had done. Now I had put fear into him and I relished the thought.

My father's psychological and emotional abuse took on a whole different meaning and intensity. The only relief was the fact that he was on the road most of the time. He was only home a few days between trips. He would be gone four to six weeks at a time on a lot of his trips. I was grounded for the rest of that summer, but I managed to sneak out to see David one more time to let him know that I was not allowed to see him again until I graduated from high school. He was terribly upset. I snuck back into the house and went up to my room. I was crying and felt empty inside. As I sat looking out of my window, David's car went speeding out of town and a few seconds later, I saw his car lights turn to the sky. He had crashed. I cannot explain all the feelings I felt at that moment. Guilt, hate for my parents, helplessness, emptiness, and a strong desire to die, were the most vivid. That night, I told God I could no longer believe in Him. I couldn't believe in a God who was supposedly loving. If He existed at all, where was He and why did He let all these awful things happen? I concluded that He did not love me, so why put any hope in Him even if He did exist. I remembered the book I was read as a child about the Devil. Now, *that* I could believe. That made sense. When I was done ranting and raving at God, I started to feel very guilty about what I had said to Him. I decided I had committed the ultimate sin by talking to Him the way I had, and He would not forgive me. I would carry that belief with me for many years to come.

The next day I found out that David and one other person were hurt in the accident but they would be all right. A few days later, one of my friends brought me a letter from David. He said he would wait for me to graduate and we would be married the day after graduation.

The rest of that summer, my mother and I got to know each other. I had wonderful friends who said I should bring my mother along with me so I could be with them. It was the only way I could go out with my friends, and that is exactly what we did. I discovered my mother was a fun-loving, caring person. We had a wonderful time with her. It got so that even when I could finally go out by myself again, my friends would ask me to bring my mother along. We even had her along when we drag-raced on the highway and when we chased cars full of boys. She would say, "You guys are nuts," and then she would laugh. I don't think my mother had ever had so much fun in her whole life. It was so good to see her laugh and giggle. We took her along to movies, on Sunday afternoon car prowls, and swimming at the lake. During this summer, my mother and I formed a strong bond. We did everything together. I talked to her about everything going on in my life. We talked about sex and what was proper to do and when. She told me that sex was for marriage only and no man wanted a woman who was not a virgin on her wedding day. You can imagine how that affected me, but she did not know what had happened to me, and what she said was her honest belief. I did not fault her for saying it, but it opened up a whole new can of worms for me.

While my father was on the road, all my friends were welcomed into our home. The more there were, the more my mother loved it. Some of my friends called her "Mom" and she thought it was great.

Even though my summer ended on a very good note, I was glad it was coming to an end and school was starting. School was the place I did most of my socializing. During the week, I was not allowed to go out unless it was school- or church-related. On weekends, I had to be in the house at nine p.m. From what my friends said, the fun did not start until after that. I decided to get involved in extra curricular activities at school. That was not as easy as it sounds since my father did not want me involved in those things. After the first time of asking, begging, and pleading, the answer was still "No," and I had to find a different approach. I knew my father did not want to look bad to anyone, so when I wanted to go out for cheerleading, I asked him for permission in front of Al and Ina. He gave me a look that could have killed but of course he said he thought it would be okay. When he got home that night, he was furious and told me to never do it again. I felt triumphant and, of course, I would do it again because it was the only way I was able to do the things I wanted to do. It did not always work, but it did work most of the time. I now had my mother on my side which also helped.

I made cheerleading that year but it had a price. Whenever my father was home and I had a game to go to, he threatened to not let me go. He and mother fought about letting me go and I felt terribly guilty about putting my mother through that. I did not miss any games, but the fun was taken away because I worried about how badly my father was treating my mother. I had seen him slap her again and I felt responsible.

The following year, I got involved in band. I was the drummer and I was good, probably because it felt good to bang on something, so I gave it all I could and thoroughly enjoyed every moment. Our band and choir director was a well-known dance band leader in our area. He had a traveling dance band which played all over the Midwest. He decided to give me free private singing lessons because he believed I had real potential as a singer. I took lessons from him for a year but decided it was not much fun. It made work out of singing. I liked to sing when it was purely spontaneous and fun. My sister and I did sing together a couple of times for an audience, but neither one of us liked to do that.

The more I excelled at anything, the more my father kept telling me how stupid I was and that I would never amount to anything. One particular morning before school, he really laid into me about it. I went to school sobbing and could not stop. My principal took me into his office and asked me to tell him what was the matter. I hesitated because the unspoken and unwritten rule in our home was that you didn't talk to anyone about what went on in the house. I finally blurted out what my father had said to me that morning. My principal proceeded to tell me he believed my father was wrong about me. He said I was a wonderful person and not to worry about getting Bs and Cs in school because I was doing the best I could, which was what really mattered. I felt better when I left his office but I was also angry with him. How dare he think I could not do better! From then on, I made the B Honor Roll. That still did not satisfy my father. He continued to compare me to my sister who was an A student. He constantly told me I would not succeed in life.

I had a lot of people who told me I was a good person and talented in many things. I tended to dismiss those things. I wanted to believe them, but somehow it was much easier to believe what my father was telling me.

15 Bible Camp

During my sixteenth summer, I was allowed to go to Bible Camp for a week with kids from my church. We were all good friends so it was great fun to be away from home and be together out from under our parents' supervision. We went to Greenlake Bible Camp which was about three hours north of home and it was a beautiful setting. The lake was clear and clean. The cabins and sleeping quarters were near the lake so at night you could hear the water lapping the shoreline. There was an area marked off for us to go swimming and they had paddle and canoe boats for us to use. The camp was set in a forest of trees and the chapel was up on a hill overlooking the camp and the lake.

The first night we were there, I spotted a boy to whom I was drawn. When I looked in his direction, my stomach did flips. The next evening, he came to talk to me while I was standing on the dock admiring the view of the lake in the moonlight. Before that night was over, he kissed me and I decided that this young man was going to be my boyfriend. I had a few guilt pangs concerning David, but not enough to stop me from wanting to be with this boy.

We were together every chance we got during the rest of that week and we had a great time together. His hometown was only about a thirty minute drive from my home so we were making plans to see each other when camp was over.

The week at camp was very special for me. The kids I went with and I built a close bond which lasted through the rest of our schooling. We had memories of that week that only we could share. I came back from camp wanting to be very involved in the church or some sort of missionary work. I decided that when I graduated from school, I would go to the seminary in Minneapolis and study to be a missionary. This was short-lived, however, because my father thought it was a crazy idea and he would not fund it.

Now that I was sixteen, I was able to start dating boys. I told my mother about the boy I met at camp and that we wanted to see each other for the rest of the summer. She said she would have to meet him before I would be allowed to date him. Both of my parents met him the following week and they both approved. I believe the fact that he was going to California in the fall for college had a lot to do with why they let me date him.

By the end of summer, I was in love with him and it was very difficult to see him leave for college. We called each other once a week and tried to write each day. He came home for the Christmas holidays and we were able to see each other then.

16 Ambivalence

On New Year's Eve of 1961, I baby-sat for a family which

had two children. The man was the son of a prominent family in town. He was also a teacher in our school. I did not have him for a teacher in any of my classes, however.

When I arrived at his home, his wife was already at the party they were invited to. He showed me that he stocked the refrigerator with beer and liquor. He told me to help myself. It was New Year's Eve and he didn't mind if I drank after I put the kids to bed. He came home at ten-thirty to see if everything was all right. He looked into the refrigerator, noticed I had not touched the alcohol, took out a bottle of beer, opened it and gave it to me. He said for me to go ahead and drink it. "Have a good time," he said. An hour later, he came home again and this time he tried to rape me. Fighting him did not stop him. When I said I heard the kids, he quit his attack and quickly left. I could not leave the kids there alone, so I stayed until both he and his wife came home an hour later. He insisted on taking me home, even though I wanted to walk home by myself. He drove me home and on the way, he begged me to not tell anyone what he had tried to do to me. I didn't tell anyone, not because of his request, but because I didn't think anyone would believe me. Again I wondered what I was doing to make men think they could do this to me.

In the spring, I was in our class play. That was a wonderful escape for me. The play was about the diary of a girl. It contained many dream scenes. We did not have all the special lighting effects which are now available to help such a venture, so the actress had the difficult task of getting these scenes across to the audience. I had the lead part in this play and totally buried myself in the part. When I was on stage practicing, and during the performances, I *was* the girl I was portraying in the play. I totally took on her personality and her mind set. I found another escape for myself! All I had to do was pretend I was someone else. I realized after each performance that I could not remember the performance. It was as if someone else had been on that stage saying the lines and acting.

I received many compliments on my performances. Apparently I was a very good actress. The night my parents came to the play, I asked my father if he had enjoyed it. By now I should have known better than to do such a thing but I still hoped someday I would do something to please him. His comment was that it was a stupid play. Since he did not call me stupid, I decided my acting must have been good.

My mother was working part-time at the Gamble Store and by the time my Junior Prom came around, she had saved enough money to buy me a beautiful dress. The day of Prom, my father was actually decent to me and acted as if he was genuinely glad I was going. I looked very pretty when I was all ready to go. He let me get to the door and put my hand on the door knob and then he said he had decided I should not go to Prom. I stopped dead in my tracks in disbelief, turned to him and asked why. My mother asked why. He said I forgot to clean something in the house that day. I started to cry. My mother was shouting at him by this time and asking him how he could be so cruel. Finally I heard her say that I was going and she told me to leave. I dashed out of the door as fast as I could so my father could not stop me. I don't know what happened between the two of them after I left. All I know is it spoiled Prom for me that year. I arrived there in tears, and I left early because I was worried about what my father might have put my mother through while I was gone.

My boyfriend came home from college for the summer of 1962 and we spent every day together that we could. I was seventeen! I was allowed to go to a couple of movies in the next town with him, which was about a twenty minute drive. It was the closest place that had a theater. While dating, I had to be home by ten p.m. which limited going very far from home. We decided to spend most of our time out at the lake. We drove on a hilly gravel road which wound its way around one part of the lake to a rest area on a hill overlooking the lake and we parked there for hours. It was during this summer that my boyfriend and I became sexually active. I did not feel good about this and my mother's voice was constantly in my head. I decided I would marry this boy because of what we were doing. I thank God that I did not get pregnant because we used no protection. He asked me if he was my first, and of course, I told him yes. I certainly could not tell him about my father. If I believed what my mother told me, he would drop me like a rock. In late August, he went back to California to continue his education. We wrote to each other every day and talked on the phone whenever we could.

I was very excited to be going into my senior year of school. Nine more months and my life would be my own. I would not have to listen to my father anymore. That sounded both fantastic and scary at the same time. I knew what to expect from him, but I did not know what to expect out there in the world by myself. I don't remember a whole lot of my senior year except counting the days until I graduated. I went to the Post Office every day during my lunch hour to get the mail in hopes that there was a letter from my boyfriend.

Our senior class planned to take a trip to Winnipeg, Canada. My father tried everything in his power to keep me from going on this trip, but in the end, my principal won out. He got the funding for me to go and insisted that my father let me go. We took the train there and had a wonderful time. After arriving, we checked into a hotel and for the next two days, we did a lot of sight-seeing. It was a fantastic time for all of us.

My sister got married in April of 1963. My father went all out and did it up right. We had the reception and dance in Mankato at Michael's. I got drunk that night and it was the second time I could not remember what I had done after drinking.

I was now eighteen and considered an adult by the world, but not by my parents. I went to my Senior Prom and wore the bridesmaid dress I had worn at my sister's wedding. I still had to be home immediately after the dance which I thought was ridiculous, but I was living under my parents' roof and they were still feeding me, so I followed their rules. I did have a wonderful time at this Prom. We all realized that we would be on our own in another month. We talked about our dreams and aspirations. Most of the girls were hoping to be married soon after graduation. A couple of them wanted to go to college. The four boys in the class were either going into the service or to college.

A couple of weeks before graduation, my parents took me to the Cities to an employment office. My father said I had to find a job and a place to live. He had already decided where I was to live so he took me there for an interview and to have me look over the place. It was a Girl's Club in downtown Minneapolis. It was like a college dormitory, and I would share a room with another girl. The rooms were very small, and there were community bathrooms and a main dining hall.

There was an eleven o'clock curfew. If we were not home at the right time for meals, we did not eat. This was not any better than living at home, but it was my way out and freedom from my father. I found a job on the second trip we made to the Cities and I was to start it on the Monday after graduation.

We were all excited and nervous on graduation day. The tears were flowing as we realized that some of us were leaving town and we would not see each other for long periods of time. I was one of fourteen in my graduating class. There were ten girls and four boys, so you can understand that we were a pretty close-knit group. After the graduation ceremony, we all stood in a reception line to be congratulated. David had come and as he approached me, I noticed my boyfriend's parents directly behind him. He looked at me as though he expected me to say something to him. I wanted to tell him that I would like to talk to him, but with the others behind him, I didn't dare.

On graduation night, I was allowed to go to a party the kids in my class were having. I was hoping that David would be there. I don't know what I expected to happen if I saw him and talked to him, but deep down inside I was hoping he would come and take me away with him. It was the last opportunity I had to speak with him and it did not happen. I stayed at the party as long as I could. I had to be home by twelve-thirty that night which also made no sense to me. After all, in three days I would be on my own in Minneapolis and yet I could not stay out with my friends as long as I wanted to on our last night together.

I packed my clothes and personal belongings that weekend and by Sunday night I was in my new home in the Cities.

Before my parents left that day, my father told me they were going to visit Germany for a few weeks, and I could not come home until they got back. If I needed any help, I was to call my sister.

Chapter 3 - Decisions

17 On My Own

I started my job as a Calculating Officer on the Monday after graduation. I liked my job and the people with whom I worked. I hated where I was living and, within a few weeks, I moved into an apartment with two of the girls from the Girl's Club. My boyfriend came back from California for the summer and found a job in the city so we could see each other all the time. He lived with one of his cousins.

During this summer, I started drinking alcohol along with my roommates and my boyfriend. The first time after drinking a bottle of beer, I began crying hysterically and saying that no one loved me, and no one cared. My boyfriend said he loved me, but to myself I thought all he cared about was sex. I learned one thing that night—booze allowed me to say what I really felt. The next morning, I felt embarrassed at the way I had acted. I decided to keep myself in better check if I was going to drink.

That summer, my boyfriend asked me to marry him and we became engaged. By the end of August, he had to leave to go back to California for school and I stayed in Minneapolis. One day at the end of August, while my friends and I were at work, our apartment was robbed. I no longer felt safe there, so I moved in with a girl from work. She lived in an apartment on Lake Calhoun with six other girls, but there was room for one more. I enjoyed living there. We were right on the beach and it was a quiet neighborhood. We constantly had something going on and drinking was not allowed in our apartment. That was important to me because I was having a difficult time controlling my drinking. Each time I drank, I began to crave more and more alcohol, so it was better that I did not drink at all.

By the end of September, my fiancé asked me to go to California with him. I did not want to do that. My job was going well, I liked where I lived, and my life seemed pretty good. He kept at me about it over the next couple of weeks. He said he found a place for us to live and the college had a job for me. When I still refused, he said he would quit college and come back to Minnesota. I could not let him do this because his father did not like me and if my fiancé quit college to come back here, I would be blamed for ruining his life. I didn't need that. He said I had to come out there or he would come home. I gave notice at work and they offered me a big raise if I would stay, but I turned it down. They said I was the best Calculating Officer they had ever employed and, if for some reason, things did not work out for me in California, they would be happy to have me come back. By the end of October, I was on a Greyhound bus to California. I did not recognize how my fiancé had manipulated me. In my immaturity, I believed he loved me so much he did not want to be without me.

18 California

I arrived in Los Angeles in four days instead of three. I stayed over in Denver for one night. I got drunk on the bus going out. There were three young people my age on the bus and we all sat together. After we had left Nebraska, a man who sat close to us offered us alcohol. We all drank until we arrived in Denver. When we stopped at a rest stop, I was terribly sick and they did not let me back on the bus. The bus company put me up in a hotel for the night and I would need to catch the next day's bus to continue my trip. I blacked out before they ever got me to my room. When they woke me in the morning, there was blood in the sink, on a towel hanging over a chair, and on the bedding. I thought maybe I had fallen and hurt myself, but I had no cuts or bruises anywhere. I told the management, and asked if they knew what had happened. They did not.

My fiancé and a friend of his were at the bus station to pick me up. I still did not feel good and must have looked like death warmed over. All I wanted to do was get to where we were going so I could take a shower and get cleaned up.

We drove to the college in Thousand Oaks. My fiancé took me to the girls' dorm, introduced me to three girls in a room and said I could clean up there and he would pick me up in a little while. I thought this was pretty strange since he said he had found a place for us to live. When he picked me up, he told me that he did not have a place for us to live! I would have to stay in the dorms with the girls until we could find a place, and the college administration could not know I was staying there. He also told me the college did not have a job for me right away.

I had spent every penny I had for the trip to California and he didn't have any money either. I wanted to turn around and go back to Minneapolis but I had no way of doing that. He took me back to the dorm that night and I talked to the girls about the situation. They said everything would be okay. They would bring me food from the commissary every day and I could stay there until I found a job and a place to live.

November 8, 1963, eight days after I arrived in California, my fiancé and I went out partying with his friends. We all decided to drive down to Tijuana so he and I could get married. We were intoxicated as we headed down the freeway. When we came back hours later, we were married. We had fifty cents to our name and still nowhere to live. Two weeks later, the college found out I was living in the dorm. They called me into the office and told me I could not stay there any longer. For the next week, I slept in my husband's car while he was still living in the dorm.

The people who owned a motel in town heard about us. They got in touch with someone at the college to tell us to come and see them. They were willing to have us stay in one of their units until we could get on our feet, and they would have us pay only what we could. I asked them why they wanted to do such a thing for us, and the woman told us she and her husband had a beginning very similar to ours until someone had helped them. They wanted to return the favor by helping someone who needed it. I was very grateful to have a place to put my belongings and a bed to sleep in. I got a job at the college as a PBX Operator. It was part time but it was a beginning. My husband also found a job in one of the grocery stores. Things were looking up.

In December, I found out I was pregnant! Our parents did not yet know we were married. Instead of telling them, we called them to ask if we could come home over the holidays to get married. Well, you would have thought World War III just broke out! His folks were calm about it compared to mine, but they did not think it was a good idea. My father told me to get my behind back to Minnesota or he would come out and get me himself. I told him he could not do that as I was eighteen and he had no say over what I did. All we wanted was a church wedding with our families present. The answer was no. I was angry and hurt. I remembered the beautiful wedding he had given my sister and I knew he would not do the same for me. We called our families back at Christmas to tell them we had gotten married in Tijuana a month earlier, and that we were now expecting a baby. There was no more yelling or screaming from our families.

A week before Christmas, we rented and moved into a small motor home. It sat in the owner's yard. We had some very good times and some very bad times in that little place. Like any newly married couple, my husband and I had our arguments. It was always about his going out with his friends and leaving me alone. I didn't like being left alone so much.

In January, we were told that our marriage was not legal because we did not register it in a United States court. Because of the fights we were having, I was in a dilemma. This was a possible way out for me. I did not like the way he was treating me and I was not at all sure I wanted to remarry him in a church. I thought about calling it quits and going back to Minnesota. I left him for a few days and stayed with a friend to think about it. The bottom line was that I could not give my father the satisfaction of thinking I had messed up my life. I also believed that if I changed toward my husband and gave him the freedom to go out when he wanted without complaining about it, things would change for the better. So I stayed, planned our church wedding with the help of friends, dug my heels in, and proceeded to try to keep my mouth shut. My sister sent me her wedding dress and I baked our wedding cake myself. We had a good time planning our wedding together. Our friends did everything they could to help us. They gave us a couple of showers because we had nothing of our own with which to set up housekeeping—the motor home we rented had everything we needed.

Just before our wedding, we were fortunate enough to get into a one bedroom apartment by the college. Our friends helped us find furniture, and we received all we needed from them and their parents to fill our apartment. Our wedding was in February of 1964, and we were very pleased at how it all turned out. I was a bit disgusted, however, when I discovered that my husband had been drinking the day of the wedding and was pretty wasted by the time the ceremony began. Our friends had a party for us after the ceremony and we all ended up drunk that night.

We spent the next couple of days opening our gifts and being at home together. We both felt as if we could finally start our life in earnest. Everything went well for quite a while and I was content to be married and have a baby on the way. The baby scared me a little because I did not know anything about taking care of a newborn. I had done a lot of baby-sitting in high school, but the kids I sat for were older. I took care of a newborn twice and when the baby cried, I felt a feeling inside of me which frightened me so much that after the second time, I refused to baby-sit for her again. I did not know where that feeling came from nor what it really was. All I knew was that I did not like the feeling. Now I would have my own newborn to take care of, and I thought about that awful feeling I had felt in the past.

My husband seemed genuinely happy about the prospect of being a father. We weren't fighting as much anymore. He took me out with him and taught me how to play pool. We invited friends over to our house quite often to play cards. He included me in just about everything he was doing. I began to believe that I truly loved this guy. The only time we fought anymore seemed to be when we went out and both had too much to drink.

One night in April, my husband went fishing by the ocean with a friend and came home at three o'clock in the morning. I was frantic. I thought something had happened to him. By the time he came home, I was angry and yelled at him as he walked in the door. He was so drunk he could hardly stand, but he managed to hit me so hard that I fell across the bed. I could not believe he would do such a thing, especially when I was six months pregnant. Much of the past came flooding into my mind and I realized for the first time that my father always seemed to have a drink in his hand. Now, also, I began to feel very guilty that I had not confided my past to my husband. I called a friend the next day and she took me to her parent's home in Beverly Hills. I stayed there for the next week, trying to decide what I should do. I was afraid of my husband. He called me asking me to come home, and I refused. At the end of the week, he came to talk to me. He apologized and said he would never hit me again. Of course I believed him; I wanted to believe him. I went back home with him and for the next few months, I was very cautious around him because I was not sure whether I could trust him.

My past kept bothering me more and more. At the end of June, we had a terrible fight. I realized that some of my attitudes toward my husband were the result of my past. The only thing I figured I could do about that was to tell him about it. I called my minister and talked to him. He agreed to come to the house and be with me when I told my husband. Through tears and trembling, I told my husband about my father. He was very sympathetic, loving, and comforting. We talked a long time with our minister and my husband sat and held me until I calmed down. For the next couple of months, he was very kind and supportive of me.

On July 31, 1964, our son Edward was born. I had a very difficult time delivering him. I was delirious through most of the labor and, in my delirium, said terrible things to my husband. The things I said hurt him very much. Both my doctor and I told him that I did not know what I was saying at the time, nor did I remember saying them, but he did not believe us. A few hours after labor began, my doctor gave me a saddle block and delivered my baby with forceps.

After the birth, I was exhausted and refused to see my baby for the next twelve hours. He scared me to death; he was so tiny–he weighed under six pounds. I realized I did not know the first thing about taking care of him.

I had heard that when a woman has a child, something called natural instinct happens and she automatically feels a closeness to her child and knows how to take care of it. None of that happened for me. I asked a lot of questions in the hospital on how to properly care for him. I received looks from the nurses that made me feel terrible—looks that said I was stupid for not knowing what to do. I got very little help from the hospital. Basically, I was told to feed him every four hours, put him on a schedule, and bathe him once a day.

Thank God my mother came out to be with me for a couple of weeks after I was released from the hospital. During that time, she taught me much of how to care for my son. She only stayed for eight days because my father called and demanded her early return. I was still afraid to take care of my son by myself.

The next couple of weeks were alright because I had a lot of company, so I was not alone with him very much. My husband loved holding and feeding our son and he was a big help to me over that time. I saw a gentle and caring side of him which was very endearing.

I had quit working at the college a few months back because I had been offered a couple of cleaning jobs in college professors' homes. The pay was better and I would be able to take my baby with me after he was born. I went to work again two weeks after my son was born because I needed to work or we would be in financial trouble. The wife of one of my employers was wonderful to me and my son. I was able to ask her anything I needed to, and she helped me tremendously. She held and rocked him when he was fussy. I told her how upset I got whenever he cried and she told me babies just need to cry sometimes and not to worry about it unless he felt as though he had a fever. I began to relax a little more with my son.

My mother-in-law came out to be with us for a couple of weeks when my son was about three months old. That was a great blessing and relief to me. I liked her very much and we got along well. I let her take care of him as much as she wanted to as it took the strain and frustration away from me. It helped to ease the tension which was present again between my husband and me.

After my mother-in-law left, my husband and I got along well for a little while. I soon realized, however, that no matter what I did for him, it was never good enough. Old feelings welled up in me and I began to feel a lot of fear toward him, so I tried harder to please him. I thought that maybe my father had been right after all; I was no good and never would be. Now when we argued, my husband called me a whore and a slut because of what I told him about my past. He was also gone practically every night. He went out with his friends to play cards, pool, and to drink. I hated being alone with my son because I was afraid of my feelings of frustration whenever he cried. When he was fussy and nothing worked to calm him down, I felt that he did not like me. One night, out of total frustration, I took him to his crib and dropped him into it. I left the room, closed the door, and sat in the living room sobbing, holding my hands over my ears to drown out his crying. I sat there until he stopped crying and fell asleep. I felt like I wanted to hit him and was glad that I controlled myself enough to not do that. I could not believe I even contemplated doing such a thing.

19 Physical or Mental

Shortly after our son was born, I began to have terrible abdominal pains which took my breath away. After a few weeks, I finally went to the doctor to get a checkup. He did all the testing he could and concluded the pain must be psychological because he found nothing physically wrong. (I have to tell you that even to this day, I usually go to the doctor only when it is too late and I end up in the hospital. I do not believe male doctors know what they are doing where women are concerned. The fact that the medical field is called "medical practice" says it all to me.) My doctor's diagnosis turned out to be a blessing in disguise for me, however. He made arrangements for me to be an outpatient at the Camarillo State Hospital, and I went twice a week. One session was spent alone with a therapist and the next session was in group therapy. I talked about everything I had been through growing up, and talked about sharing this with my husband, his reaction, and how he had treated me since that time.

After a few sessions at the hospital, the pains in my abdomen grew stronger and came more often. The therapist wanted my husband to come to the group sessions. He said we should go to a couple's group. It took me days before I could convince him to come. During our session together, he was asked if he had done and said the things I had told them he had. He admitted he had, and tried to excuse his behavior by blaming me. Everyone came down on him so hard that I, in my codependency, felt sorry for him. They told me to stop bailing him out by accepting the blame for everything he did. Needless to say, my husband refused to go back to counseling with me. The next session, I went without him and was told in no uncertain terms that I would not be able to get healthy until I left my husband because he was mentally abusive, violent and, worst of all, he was not willing to look at himself to change his behavior. I refused to listen. I believed that if I only loved him enough, things would get better.

In August of 1965, on a Sunday morning, my husband took me to the hospital because I could not stand the pain any longer. As soon as we walked into the hospital, I fainted from the pain. When I awoke, I was told they had done exploratory surgery and found a cyst the size of a golf ball on my ovary. My doctor told me that since they had me open, they also took out my appendix, so I would have no reason for any more pain. He did not want me to get pregnant for at least three, and preferably six, months so that everything could heal properly.

Two months later, I found out I was pregnant. I had been taking birth control pills regularly and could not understand how this could happen. My husband flew into a rage and accused me of getting pregnant on purpose. Then he decided it was not his child! The bottom line was that he didn't want the responsibilities he already had, and he certainly did not want any more. This, of course, was also a good excuse for him to continue to go out with his friends whenever he wanted to. I decided to totally concentrate on my son and to basically try to stop caring about my husband. That made my life easier as I was not so consumed with what my husband was doing. It seemed to confuse him, because shortly after that, he began to be home more often and he was very attentive to me.

I continued to go to therapy because it was helping me with caring for my son. My son was now a year old and during my therapy, I talked about my frustrations with him and the fact that I had already slapped his hands and spanked him. I told them I felt terrible about this and did not want to continue these actions. It reminded me of the way my father treated me and I did not want to treat my own child in that way. The therapist and my group were not judgmental and offered me many alternatives to use when my frustration level would get the better of me. I did what they suggested and I was able to relax enough to occasionally sit down and play with my son. Before, it seemed as though raising him was only a serious job I had undertaken. It was strictly business and I had not allowed myself to enjoy my little boy. I had, in effect, been given permission by my therapist and my group to play with my son. Since adults did not play with me when I was a child, my subconscious attitude was that raising kids was not supposed to be fun.

We moved into a two-bedroom apartment in the same complex in which we were living. It was wonderful having a room for our son. He was full of energy and so eager to learn about everything he saw. There was more room for him to play and we didn't feel so crowded. He was a happy little boy except at bedtime. Right from the very beginning, he cried when he was put down at night. I hated putting him to bed because of his crying. One day, during a therapy session, someone suggested a night-light, thinking that perhaps he was afraid of the dark. I had tried everything else I could think of and had taken suggestions from others of what to do and nothing had worked. The night-light was, however, exactly what it took for him to stop crying when put to bed at night. The poor little guy did not like the dark.

While I was in therapy, my father called me to tell me he and my mother were getting divorced and it was all my fault because I had left home. I talked about this in my sessions and it was suggested that I needed to let my mother know what had happened to me so that she could use this information to her advantage if she needed to. A few days later, I called my sister to find out what was going on with the divorce. She told me our father was being very nasty and trying his best to leave my mother with nothing. He was trying to get people to believe that my mother was insane. I was determined to not let him get away with this. He had abused all of us enough; now I would do whatever I needed to in order to stop it. My sister wanted to know what I thought I could do, and I told her that I was going to tell mother something which would change his attitude. I then called my father and told him I would come home and go to court with Mom if he made it necessary. I also called my mother and told her all about the sexual abuse. My father backed off and things did not end up as bad for my mother as they could have been otherwise.

20 Arizona

In January of 1966, my husband quit college and took a job with the Motorola Company in Phoenix, Arizona. We packed everything we owned into a small U-Haul trailer and moved to Arizona. We stayed in a dingy little place for a couple of weeks and then found a nice house to rent. At first we really liked Arizona. My husband and I were getting along very well because we did not know anyone in Phoenix so we had only each other. He was home every night and I felt as though we were finally living the way a family should. I was also having a wonderful time with my son. He and I went for a lot of walks, we sat for hours playing together, and every two weeks, when the city irrigated the yards, we went out into the backyard and played in the water. I was much more relaxed and truly began to enjoy my life. My husband and I got involved in a pool tournament, and being very pregnant and not very agile when it came to reaching across the pool table to shoot a ball, I did quite well and made it to the finals before I bombed out.

My husband was working with chemicals at his job, one of which was cyanide. He began to get a terrible rash on his hands and forearms. After a while, medications didn't touch it, and he needed to think about quitting his job for the sake of his health. By May, neither of us was very happy there anymore. His reaction to the chemicals was getting to him. He could hardly get a decent night's sleep because of terrible itching. The weather became unbearably hot and made me miserable in my pregnancy. (One hundred and thirteen degrees Fahrenheit in the shade is a bit much for anyone.)

One morning when I went out to the kitchen to make breakfast, I saw a huge bug on the kitchen floor. I screamed for my husband to come and get it out of the house. I kid you not, that bug was at least three inches long, orange, and hard shelled. I also heard that a rattler had been on a woman's porch only a few blocks away from our house the day before. When the woman tried to get it off of her porch with a broom, it attacked her and she was now in the hospital. I told my husband I wanted to go back to Minnesota NOW! He tried to get me to wait a few more weeks before making that decision because he had a chance to change jobs within the company. I absolutely refused, and told him I was leaving as soon as I could get everything packed. He could come with me or he could stay, but I was going home. I called my husband's parents and told them we were coming home. They said we could stay with them until my husband found a job and we could find a place to live. They were excited about getting acquainted with their grandson and being able to have him there for a while. Two weeks later, we were on our way back to Minnesota. We had been told our baby was due at the end of July, and I was glad I was going to be back home to deliver this time.

Chapter 4 - Better Off Without Me

21 Coming Home

We were only home a few days when my husband, my son, and I went to see Charlie. Charlie was the man who had been paying for my husband's college education. I met Charlie for the first time when he came to visit us while we lived in Arizona. He was a very kind and gentle man, and had known my husband from the time of his birth. He bought us a brand new car when we lived in California. Charlie and our son were best of friends right away, and it was apparent that he loved children.

Charlie lived a half a block away and across the street from my husband's parents' home. He was in his sixties and had been a bachelor all his life. A couple of big dogs kept him company, and they were really his family. One of his dogs had recently died and Charlie put his body into his freezer because he had not yet decided what he wanted to do with it. As he talked about his dog, tears came to his eyes, for he had truly lost a friend. We visited for quite a while and I enjoyed talking with this man. He had done so much for us and I was grateful.

It became bluntly apparent that my husband's parents did not like our association with Charlie. There seemed to be a terrible animosity between them. I could not understand it. After all, this man was putting their son through college. It seemed to me they could be a little grateful, but they were not.

In July, my husband decided he would go back to California to finish school. He said he could do this as Charlie would take care of us financially. I did not like the idea, but went along with it. I did tell him I would not live with his parents for a year. Our baby was due and we did what we could to have it born before he left. We walked a lot and one night we even jogged a while, but it only resulted in false labor. My husband left for California the last week of July.

I went to visit Charlie almost every day after my husband left. He told me many things he had done with my husband during his growing up years. He had been a friend of the family at one time and took my husband on many fishing, hunting, and other trips. I knew Charlie had taken him to Alaska a few years earlier. His involvement with my husband was strongly resented by my husband's family and it had been for many years. I wondered why his family didn't put a stop to it if they did not like it.

I wanted to get to know Charlie better so I asked him many questions about what he had done in his life. He was a soldier in France during World War II and afterwards, he worked for the railroad until he retired. I asked why he never married, especially since he loved kids so much. He took me into his attic and dug into a lockbox. He showed me a huge diamond engagement ring. He had been in love at one time, but it did not work out. He still seemed sad about it, so I did not ask him anything more about it. Charlie then told me there were some legal papers he wanted to make sure my husband received when he died. I was to make sure that he got them. They were in the lockbox and contained things about which he wanted my husband to know. I relayed all of this to my husband some time later.

My in-laws were not happy that I was spending so much time with Charlie. I did not need them to decide who I should associate with. I liked Charlie and so did my son. Other things were being said which hurt and were very upsetting. I decided it was time to move out of there as quickly as I could. I moved into an apartment with my mother. She and my sister were living in a small town south of the Twin Cities. I was glad to be with my family again. I wrote to my husband every day and we called each other often. We had been getting along well for over seven months and I really missed him.

At six o'clock in the morning on August 31, 1966, my sister drove me to the hospital to have my baby. She had to be somewhere that morning and absolutely could not stay with me past seven o'clock. Remembering the difficult time I had delivering my son, I was very nervous about being left alone. I gave birth to a beautiful, four-pound, fifteen-ounce baby girl an hour and a half after my sister left. It was a "piece of cake" delivering this time. I called everyone I knew as soon as I got to my room. My in-laws came to see me the next day. My mother, who was taking care of my son, came with my sister. My husband called and we had no trouble deciding on our baby's name. Charlie came the day we were to be released. He held the baby as if he held babies all the time. There was no awkwardness at all. When I was ready to leave the hospital, I was told the bill had been taken care of by Charlie.

Eddie was fascinated with his tiny sister, Marie. He wanted to hold her all the time and did not like to hear her cry. She was so small that I bathed her in a mixing bowl the first couple of weeks. I had to feed her every three hours because of her size. She slept so well that I woke her for most of her feedings. She didn't seem to have a time of day when she was fussy, either. After we had been home for just a few days, Eddie came down with tonsillitis. He was terribly sick for three days. I was up with him day and night just trying to keep his fever down, but on the third day it finally broke. Because of the worrying and lack of sleep, I no longer had enough milk to satisfy Marie, so I quit nursing. She did very well on formula and gained weight rapidly. It was nice having my mother there with me. She did most of the cleaning and cooking so I could concentrate on my children. After about a month, she and I started to get on each others' nerves, which is pretty normal. (They say you can not go home again after you have been out on your own for a while).

Five weeks after Marie was born, I called my husband and told him I wanted him to come home. We could move to Mankato and he could go to college there. I told him we needed him with us and he must either come back or our marriage was over. He did come back a week later. He found a job in a small town a few miles from us and we stayed where we were for a short time.

22 Mankato

We moved to Mankato after my husband found a job there, an apartment on South Fourth Street, and had registered at Mankato State University to finish his education. He had changed his major to Psychology, and it would take him much longer to finish. He definitely resented the fact I had asked him to come back from California. He was gone all the time and we fought constantly. I was also getting phone calls from women for him, but they never left their names. My husband said the calls were from people he was tutoring at school. I didn't buy that for a minute. If it was true, they surely would not hesitate to leave their names. I was very unhappy and I seemed to have very little patience with Eddie again.

Thirty years ago, no one I knew disagreed with spanking as a form of discipline. My definition of a spanking was to hit on the butt hard enough to give a child the impression that you mean business, but not hard enough to bruise or cause injury. I did not like spanking, however, because of how it made me feel. So most of the time I screamed at my son. I did not want my son to be afraid of me. However, I occasionally spanked him and yelled at him so much that he did become afraid of me. During the next few months, Eddie became very insecure and never knew how I would react to anything he did. One minute I laughed with him because of something he was doing, and ten minutes later I yelled at him for the very same thing. I was no longer mentally stable and the child could not count on any stability in his life.

From the time my husband returned from California until February of 1967, our relationship had gotten as bad as I thought it could get. He told me many times that I was no good and that he and the children would be better off without me. After months of his psychological abuse, I began to believe him. I believed that the best thing for everyone, including myself, was for me to no longer exist. One night when he started another terrible fight with me, I decided to commit suicide. (He started fights frequently so he could justify leaving the house to go drink or whatever he was doing by then.) I told him if he left I would kill myself. He laughed and told me to go ahead but he was not worried because I wouldn't have the guts to do it. He left.

23 Suicide Attempt

There was a bottle of liquor in the house so I poured myself a full glass and went into the bathroom to get all the pills I could find. A couple of months earlier I had gone to the doctor because I could not sleep and was terribly nervous. He prescribed sleeping pills and tranquilizers for me. I sat down at the dining room table, poured out all the pills I had left and proceeded to count them. I wanted to make sure there were enough to do the job. I counted eight sleeping pills, sixteen tranquilizers, and forty-one aspirins. That was all I had in the house. I sat and cried and drank straight whiskey until the bottle was almost gone and then I took the pills by the handfuls until they were gone.

The girlfriend I had all through school was living in Mankato at the time, and we were still very close. When we were in high school, she confided to me that her father also sexually abused her, so we had a special bond between us. As I started to get really drowsy–to the point where I could hardly stand up–I called her to say good-bye. I talked with her only for a minute because she could not understand what I was trying to say. I learned afterward that she called our house until she got an answer from my husband. She told him what she had been able to understand me say.

I have no idea what time my husband came home that night. I vaguely remember being held up by him in the bathroom. He was making me drink soapy water which made me vomit. After a couple of swallows, I refused to take anymore and he put me to bed. This was on a Saturday night. The next time I came to, it was Tuesday. The very first feeling I had when I woke up was anger because I was still alive. I could not even do this right! I tried to get up but my legs would not support my body. They felt numb and I lay back down. My husband came into the room, looked at me and said, "Don't you ever do this to me again." I do not have the words to describe the rage I felt at that moment. I said things to him I could not write here or anywhere. In essence, I told him to get out of my face as I did not care if I ever saw him again, and to get my mother to come to help me. My mother came that day and she said she would stay with me as long as I needed her. During the week she was with me, I resolved that I would never again allow any man to make me feel so awful about myself that I would try to take my life. Where my husband was concerned, I shut my feelings off. From then on, whenever he put me down or criticized me, I flung it right back at him. It did not solve anything, but I got my feelings of anger out.

The first week after my suicide attempt, it became very clear to me that God must be looking out for me. There wasn't any reason for me to be alive considering the amount of alcohol and pills I had taken. I decided that if He wanted me alive so badly, then I'd better get myself some help so I could get strong enough to want to live. I certainly did not want to be alone with my husband again, because not only did I not love him, I did not even like him anymore. So I called my medical doctor and told him what I had done and that I wanted help. He said the amount of stuff I had taken should have killed a person twice my size. I only weighed eighty-five pounds. He believed I most likely was in a coma during those three days I was supposedly sleeping. He could not understand how my husband had let me lie there without taking me to the hospital. He understood that I wanted help and called the hospital to check me into the mental ward for psychiatric help.

I stayed in the hospital for a couple of weeks. I did not like the psychiatrist I was given. He didn't sit down and talk to me. All he did was pump me full of drugs and come in once a day to ask me how I was feeling. I shared a room with another girl. One morning I woke up and was shaking uncontrollably. An alarm went off, the nurses came running in to the room and immediately made me drink orange juice. I stopped shaking almost instantly. When they left, I asked my roommate about this and she told me they had given me an insulin shot during the night and I had experienced insulin shock. I was furious. No one had asked me for permission and they were not supposed to do anything to me without my knowledge since I voluntarily admitted myself. When I confronted the psychiatrist about this, he walked over to my roommate and slapped her for telling me what he had done. I told him to not come near me again and to immediately release me. My husband came that day to get me and when he did, the psychiatrist told him that I would never be well. According to him, I would be hospitalized at least once a year from then on and my husband had to decide whether he could live with that.

After two days of being home, I felt like a caged lion. I did not want to be there and I did not want to be with my husband–he disgusted me. I wanted to be in a safe place where I did not have to look at or deal with him. There was a lot going on inside of me and I had no idea how to deal with it. I needed help and I knew it. My doctor called the Glenwood Hills Mental Hospital in Minneapolis and got me in right away. My husband put our children with people who ran a foster home in his hometown because he had no idea how long I would be gone. My son was two and a half years old and my daughter was six months old. I would not see them for the next two and a half months.

The psychiatrist assigned to me at Glenwood Hills was a kind, compassionate, and gentle man. I found him easy to talk to. I had sessions with him three times a week and group therapy every day. He put me on antidepressants to settle me down so that I could begin to deal with my problems. When we began to look at my past life, I found that I had been preoccupied with thoughts of death because of the incest. My psychiatrist believed I subconsciously tried to kill myself when I fell off those bridges on the way to school in Germany, and that I consciously wanted to kill myself when I threw the brick into the air so it could land on my head.

When I was a teenager, I did things that put me on the edge between life and death. I swam across the lake on the outskirts of town, believing ahead of time that I could not make it across. I did make it however! I rode motorcycle with a boy who raced them professionally. We rode in and out of the white center lines of the highways at 60 to 70 miles per hour. When I was allowed to drive our car, I drag raced on the highways and jumped across highways, coming off of gravel roads at a high rate of speed and sending the car flying to the other side of the road. I thought all of this was thrilling and never gave a thought to dying. I wasn't afraid of dying. I was afraid of living.

About three weeks into my therapy, my psychiatrist told me that I had every right to be angry with my father. He understood why I felt so much hate for him. He suggested that I call him and tell him to pay my hospital bill since I was there as a direct result of his abuse. I called him and told him exactly that and he hung up on me. From then on, I consciously blamed him for everything that was wrong in my life. I took very little responsibility for the way my life was going. I believed it was all due to him, and I was the victim of circumstances. I believe my psychiatrist said what he did concerning my father with my best interest in mind. I took his statement about hating my father as permission to continue that hate. For the next twelve years, I had no contact with my father.

We talked about the abuse I received from my husband. He told me that no one deserved to be treated in an abusive manner, but I had to be the one to put an end to it in any way I thought necessary. He said that if the abuse did not stop, I would not be able to stabilize my life and deal with the issues I needed to deal with.

We discussed how rough I thought I had treated my son and the feeling of frustration I felt and how that feeling seemed to have its own identity apart from me. I wanted help to get rid of that feeling or at least channel it in different directions. He told me it was not wrong to spank a child when the child had done something wrong. It was wrong, however, to spank him only out of my own frustration. He suggested I count to ten before I touched him. That would give me some time to decide whether a situation really warranted a spanking. He suggested I put him in his room for a cooling off period instead of spanking him. He told me I should not be so hard on myself because I had done all I could to learn better ways of handling my son. He did not know of any parent who did not periodically spank or yell at their children. My trouble was that I wanted to be the perfect parent and when I realized that I was not, my frustration with myself got the better of me. All of this understanding and compassion should have helped me to feel better about how I treated my son, but it didn't. I wanted to be fixed so I would not have that feeling of frustration again because when I had it, it felt like I was walking on the edge of a cliff, not knowing if, or when, I would go over the edge.

After a month, I was able to leave the hospital for weekend visits. My husband came to the Cities for the weekends and we spent them together in my mother's apartment. She lived in the Cities at that time and was working for families who were on vacations. She took care of the children while the parents were away. My husband brought lots of liquor with him each weekend. We basically stayed in the apartment, tried to talk through our problems and we drank! Obviously we did not work through much of anything. After another six weeks in the hospital, I felt strong enough to leave and go home. I believed I had worked through enough of my problems to be able to take on being a mother and wife again. I was referred to a psychiatrist in Mankato and was to see him every two weeks. After I saw him a couple of times the first week I was home, he put me on more medication. I walked around as if I were in a fog most of the time because of this.

The day after I came home from the hospital, my in-laws brought my children home to me. Eddie was almost three now and Marie was nine months old. My son walked in the door, looked around the apartment, looked at me, turned to his grandmother and said, "I want to go home." I started to cry. My mother-in-law tried to assure me that the surroundings were unfamiliar to him because he had not been home for three months. I knew differently. I recognized fear and apprehension when I saw it, and it tore my heart out. I vowed to myself I would be a better mother to my son.

We settled into our home again and everything went well with the children and my husband. Over the next several months, I gained my son's trust. My children spent almost every weekend with either my sister and her family or with my mother-in-law. It was my family's way of helping so that I did not get stressed out by my children. I am so grateful to them for doing that. My children and I needed those breaks from each other at that time. It made each week much easier for me to handle.

Because of all the drugs I was on, it was very difficult for me to wake up in the mornings. When Eddie was almost four and Marie was almost two, he got up around five-thirty or six o'clock in the morning, would wake his sister, take her by the hand and go three blocks downtown to a coffee shop. After the first time, I talked to him about why he should not do that but he kept on. Four times, businessmen brought them home after they had fed my children breakfast. The only thing we could do was put locks high up on our apartment doors so my son could not open them.

One morning, Eddie crawled into bed with me and was crying. It took me a few minutes to wake up and realize he was hurt. He had stepped into the hot water of the vaporizer in his room. I pulled his pajama bottom off and his foot was full of blisters. It was five-thirty in the morning. I called our doctor at his home. His office was only two blocks away and he could meet us there right away. I grabbed both of my children and ran down to his office with them, one under each arm. I felt as if I were the most terrible mother on earth because it had taken me a few minutes to wake up and realize what had happened. It had been almost a year of seeing the psychiatrist and I wanted him to start taking me off the drugs he prescribed because I was tired of feeling like a zombie, and because I had such a hard time waking up in the mornings. He refused, so I went home and flushed all the medication down the toilet. It took about a week before I finally felt like I had a clear head.

I had allowed myself to begin to have feelings for my husband again by this time. He had been very helpful with the children and very attentive to me. Since this had been the case for a few months now, I started to trust him a little.

In 1968, we rented the main floor of a small house in lower North Mankato. Where we had been living, there wasn't a yard for the children to play in, nor anyone for them to play with. This house had a decent yard and there were a lot of children their ages in the neighborhood. Across the street from us were two huge empty lots where all the kids would get together and play. It was wonderful to be able to send my son outside and watch him have fun. We met all the neighbors who also had young children and we became friends. The women and I got together practically every day for coffee and we all sewed for ourselves and our children. My new friends were very important to me and I really enjoyed being with them. I noticed that two of these mothers were continuously spanking and yelling at their children. I felt sorry for the kids. I still spanked and yelled at mine, but not like these mothers were doing. I began to believe that perhaps I was not such an awful mother after all.

We found out that my husband's insurance was not covering all of my medical expenses. My husband had a good paying job at the Foundry and I was confident we could manage to pay it off over time. We tried to get help from Medical Assistance for two thousand dollars of the remaining bills, but my husband made ten cents an hour too much for us to qualify. He told me that since I had made the bills, I could pay them because he was not going to. My psychiatrist did not want me to go to work because he believed it would be too stressful for me. In order to stop making more medical bills, I stopped my sessions. My husband kept at me about working, until I figured the stress of him pushing me to go to work was probably worse than actually going to work. I found a job at a private supper club in town and worked from five p.m. to midnight and sometimes two o'clock in the morning, three to four nights a week. This way we did not have to hire baby-sitters for the kids. The nights my husband could not be home, his mother came to stay. I enjoyed getting out of the house and working. The tips were great and I used them to pay off my medical bills. The only drawback was that I was so tired I could hardly function on the days following the nights I worked until two a.m.

By 1968, I had not yet taken the test for my American Citizenship. In the spring, I went to the Cities to take the test and be sworn in as a citizen. I had studied for six months and knew the names of all the Senators and Representatives. I knew the Constitution, the Amendments, and the branches of the Government. The only question the examiner asked me was, "What is the Highest Court in the land?" I froze and could not think! The examiner said, "Could it be the Supreme Court?" I yelled excitedly, "That's it!" I was totally embarrassed! He smiled and swore me in as an American Citizen!

24 Assembly of God Church

I joined a Pentecostal Church in 1968 and went every

week. They talked about the Baptism of the Holy Spirit, physical and mental healing, and miracles. They said all these things were as real now as they were in Jesus' time. They talked about all the Gifts of the Spirit mentioned in the Bible. This was very intriguing to me since the Lutheran Church I attended never talked about these things. Each service ended with people coming forward and being prayed over for the Gifts of the Spirit and healing. I had just about given up receiving anything from the Holy Spirit. I remembered the way I talked to God when I was a teenager and this was confirmation that God had not forgiven me. That is when I received the Baptism. While the congregation was praying with me, I felt a peace within me the like of which I had never before felt. It was almost like the peace I felt the day of my Confirmation, only this time it was not just a feeling of serenity, it was also a knowledge of forgiveness and love. I was talking but did not recognize the words I was saying. The minister was also talking and the feeling of peace, serenity, and forgiveness kept flowing into me like a river of water washing over me. When the words I spoke stopped, the minister's words also stopped. He had interpreted what I was saying. The night this happened, my mother-in-law stayed at our house so I could go to church. When I came home I told her what had happened. She was glad for me, she said, but I could tell she thought I was probably going off the deep end again.

For some reason when I went to bed that night, I did not get undressed. I just lay down across the bed and fell asleep. I was still a very sound sleeper once I fell asleep. At two o'clock in the morning, I sat straight up as if someone had jarred me awake. I sat and listened. I heard a small whisper from the children's room. I ran in and Eddie was gasping for air. I picked him up, woke my mother-in-law, told her to call the hospital and tell them we were on our way. As we got to the first stop sign, one block away, my son whispered as he gasped for each breath, "It's okay, Mom. If I die, I will be with Jesus." To this day, I do not remember the drive to the hospital from that point on. The next thing I remember is Eddie being under a tent in a hospital bed, breathing easier. He had had a severe asthma attack that night.

My son turned four that summer and in the fall, I enrolled him in Head Start. I volunteered to help out because I knew that I could learn things from the program to help me handle myself better with my children. I was looking for ways to learn how to do things differently so I could be a better mother than I thought I was. I had been told by a number of people, including my mother-in-law, that I was a very good mother, but what mattered was that I did not feel that way. I learned a lot about myself that year. I had an unspoken belief which was that whatever my children did was a direct reflection on me. That was one reason I was so strict with them. I wanted them to be perfect little children so I would look good. I started working on dispelling this belief at that time but it took years of hard work to finally let go of it completely. The church and the spirituality I had found helped me tremendously in working on this. I was calmer with my children, and began to use better ways of disciplining them.

In the summer of 1969, one of my husband's cousins came to visit us for a few days. The first day he was there, we had a lot of fun visiting. The next evening, he and my husband sat in the living room and smoked marijuana. They kept at me to try it. I had my fill of drugs when I was under psychiatric care and I was very leery of illegal drugs. They convinced me that smoking it once would not hurt anyone. We were drinking wine along with smoking the pot. The marijuana made me see things much more vividly and I remember going to turn the television down time and time again because it seemed to keep getting louder. I thought this was very interesting and sat explaining to them what it made me feel like when all of a sudden, out of nowhere, my husband started slapping me around. He knocked me to the floor several times. I kept telling him to stop. His cousin sat there and did nothing. When he finally stopped, I ran to the bedroom and went to bed. I stayed in bed for the next three days because I was terribly sick from the wine and pot, and I did not want to be around my husband. I was totally confused by what happened. We had been getting along well for a long time. We had not been fighting or arguing very much. I decided to blame the marijuana for what happened but I was very careful around my husband for a long time after that. He promised me he would not use marijuana again.

Instead of looking to God for comfort, I began to turn away from Him once again. The stress I felt because of this incident took its toll. Whenever I felt a lot of stress, I could not eat. My weight went down to eighty pounds, I was anemic and I could not keep anything down. I ended up in the hospital being fed intravenously to get my system going again.

Eddie started kindergarten that fall and I cried the first day he went to school. He was excited to be going and waved good-bye to me as we got to the corner of the school. He did not want me to walk him inside! He learned everything very quickly and did a wonderful job in school.

Marie was three years old then and quite the little lady. She was quiet, reserved and had a totally different personality from her brother. She very seldom did anything wrong. When she did, all I ever needed to do was scold her. That alone made her feel so bad that she would come hug me and say she was sorry. She also played by herself a lot. She did not need to be entertained very much. She had quite an imagination for her young age and was a happy and loving little girl. She crawled up on my lap about once a day and we read a book or just snuggled. When she was done, down she would go and she would find something else to do.

Early that fall, my grandfather wrote and wanted the children and I to come back to Germany for a visit. He would pay our way. It was okay with my husband, and I was really excited about seeing him again. We were to go the following May. I made our reservations in November. In December, I started to have a terrible nightmare. It consisted of the following: We were on the plane over the ocean and the plane went down. We all ended up safely in the water. My mother had a hold of Eddie and I was holding Marie. I looked down at her and she had slipped away from me. I could not find her. I awoke in a cold sweat.

The same nightmare reoccurred every night for three weeks. I decided to cancel the reservations and as soon as I did, the nightmare stopped.

During the time we were to be in Germany, many things happened. The day we were to have left for Germany, Eddie ended up in the hospital with emergency exploratory surgery. He had terrible stomach pains and his white blood count was sky-high. When the doctors pressed on his abdomen, it did not hurt him where a normal appendix would hurt, so they did not know what it was. It turned out to be his appendix, but it was behind the bowel track instead of in front where it was supposed to be. A couple of weeks after Eddie's surgery, my husband was in the hospital to have a rapidly growing tumor on his chest removed. He was home for a couple of weeks when I ended up in the hospital with kidney problems. By the time I was well, it was the end of the time we would have spent in Germany. The only person in the family to whom nothing happened during those six weeks was Marie. Needless to say, I pay attention to dreams if the same dream keeps repeating itself. I may not understand the dream, but I have learned to heed them as warnings from a spiritual force outside of myself.

25 Our Own Home

In May of 1970, we moved into our own home, just two blocks from where we were living. Owning our own home was a dream come true and we were elated. We had a lot of fun getting our house to look and feel like a home. We did not have much extra money with which to buy things, but that was okay. We would do what we could, when we could. Six months after we bought our home, my husband and I started fighting again. Now along with my supposedly being stupid, everything that went wrong in his life was said to be my fault. He had always been very sarcastic and now sarcasm was all I heard from him. I thought I could play that game as well as he could, so I lashed back at him with the same putdowns and accusations. I was going to fight back and not buy into all his bull. Of course our relationship got worse by the week. Our children were upset all of the time and they started fighting. They had had their little squabbles before, which were nothing serious, but now it was serious, with pushing and hitting.

The worse things got, the more I yelled at them and my children were getting very hyper. The only break seemed to be the weekends they went to Grandma and Grandpa's. My husband and I tried to get along during the weekdays when Grandma would stay at our house.

Grandma worked at a grocery store in town so it was easy and very convenient for her to stay in town with us, especially on snowy days. She lived in a small town outside of Mankato and she commuted every day. During one of the nights she stayed with us, I yelled at my son for something he had done. She told me that she carried a wooden spoon with her everywhere she went when her son was small. She said she had only needed to use it on him a few times, and after that, all she needed to do was reach in her purse for it when he misbehaved and he shaped right up. That sounded good to me if it meant that I could stop spanking and yelling at my children. I went and bought myself one. After spanking with it a couple of times, all I needed to do was open the kitchen drawer where I kept it and they immediately stopped misbehaving.

Things kept escalating between my husband and me in 1971. I found a bong in his coat one day and realized he had been smoking pot all along. I told him I had had enough and wanted a divorce. I had said that to him many times before, but this time he knew I was serious. He seemed to change overnight. He stopped all the abusive language and treated me with what seemed like respect. I was not biting this time though, and still intended to divorce him–until I found out I was pregnant again. When I told him, he smiled and said he guessed we could not get a divorce now. I told him that the baby would not stop me. With that, things calmed down a lot more. He still went out a lot but I did not care anymore. I was glad when he was gone. When I wanted to go out, I went with my girlfriends. Once in a while, he and I would go out together and it was always to a bar. All through our marriage I drank periodically–once or twice a month at most. During this pregnancy, my husband and I lived in the same house but as far as I was concerned, sharing a house was all there was. I shut my feelings off and did not care what he did. The nicer he treated me, the more leery I became of him. We had gone through this before–too many times. I was not going to get sucked in again.

On August 8, 1972, Michelle was born. My husband was with me through part of the labor. He had treated me decently, almost with kindness, for quite a while and I was softening. As abusive as he had been in the past, he was not abusive in any way toward the children. He was a very loving and gentle father. So, by this time, I decided to forget about the divorce.

Our friend, Charlie, died and left half of his estate in a trust fund for the education of our children. The interest from that fund was to be paid quarterly to my husband until his death. The interest alone was quite substantial. I wanted to stay home with my children instead of working outside the home. My husband wanted me to go back to work, but I did not go back for quite a while after Michelle was born. I thoroughly enjoyed my time at home with her. Eddie and Marie were both in school full time, so this little one and I had all day together. My husband kept after me to go back to work. I saw no reason for it since the extra income from the trust fund afforded me the luxury of being home with my children. They were all doing well now and I was doing well with them. In order to get me back to work, he spent every penny from the trust on things he wanted. When I told him what the children needed, he told me to go to work so I could get it for them. I went to work in April of 1973.

The end of June, 1973, we went up north on a fishing trip with my husband's parents. We took a baby-sitter along for our youngest so we could all go fishing when we wanted to. It was a wonderful trip. It had been a long time since my husband and I genuinely had fun together. I came home from that week with hope in my heart for our relationship. We came home during North Mankato Days.

North Mankato Days is a weekend festival held at the beginning of July. There is a parade and a carnival in one of the parks. We took the kids to the carnival in the afternoon. I talked my husband into going back with me that night. He had a terrible sunburn on his legs from our trip up north and was not very comfortable, so we were not going to stay late. He had been drinking all afternoon and then we went to the Beer Garden at the carnival that evening. While I danced, he sat and drank and talked to friends. About ten-thirty he said he wanted to go home. I figured he was feeling uncomfortable because of his sunburn so I began to walk home with him. Two blocks from home I told him I would walk home with him but I wanted to go back and dance some more. He turned and started beating me. He hit me so hard that I fell to the ground. He yanked me back up and beat me some more. He pulled me along toward home and with each step he hit me. A half a block from our home, I saw the neighbors come out on their porch to see what was going on as I was yelling for someone to call the police. My husband saw them as they went back into their house. He stopped hitting me and pulled me along with him. From that point to the time we reached our house, I convinced him to walk the baby-sitter home because I did not want her to see me like this. I told him I would wait outside until they left. My eyes were swelling shut and I felt blood running down my face. My whole body ached. As soon as he left with the baby-sitter, I went inside, locked all the doors, and called the police. I told them I needed someone there immediately as I had been beaten and he would be back in a few minutes. I hung up, turned around, and my son was there. He hugged me and said he did not want me to let his father back in the house. I told him not to worry, I would take care of everything. I sent him back to bed. The police came in less than two minutes, but those minutes seemed like an eternity. I told them what happened and they waited for my husband to come back. When he did, he strolled into the house as if nothing was wrong, sat down and asked why the police were there. His shirt was spattered with my blood and his hands were bloody. They asked him if he had beaten me. He said if I said he had, he must have. The police told him to get his things because he could not stay there. When he protested, they told him he either had to leave and not come back until I said he could or they would take him to jail. He argued with them for a while, first in the house, then outside. He finally left. I called a girlfriend to come and stay with me that night because I was afraid he would come back.

The next day I went to the police station to file a report and have pictures taken of my face and the bruises on my body. The following day, I went to an attorney and filed for a divorce. My mother-in-law came to stay with me for a few days because I was afraid. She was very supportive of me. She said she did not blame me for filing for divorce as I did not deserve to be treated the way her son had treated me.

My father-in-law came by to see me that week. He asked me what I had done to get such a beating. It took all that was inside of me to not throw him out of the house. I looked at him and said that no one deserved to be beaten, no matter what they had done, and left it at that.

I was employed at a pizza place in town. I called my boss, told him what had happened and that I could not go back to work the way I looked and I did not know how long it would take for me to heal. He said to come back when I was ready. Two weeks later, I went back even though my face was still black and blue. After a couple of days of working, I realized I was so upset that I was not able to do a good job. I talked to my boss again and told him I needed to quit because I was too upset to think about anything but my upcoming divorce. He understood.

CHAPTER 5 - ALONE WITH CHILDREN

26 Divorced

There were two reasons I stayed in my marriage as long as I did. First, I felt if we broke up, it would be my failure, and second, even when we did not get along, I hoped that it would be good someday if I just hung in there. That may not make any sense but it is why I stayed.

About a week after the beating, my husband called and said he wanted to talk. I refused and said I was not yet ready to talk and I did not know when I would be. I told him I had filed for a divorce. He kept calling and a week later, I agreed to meet with him at a restaurant to talk. He said he did not remember the night he beat me up, nor beating me up. He was sorry and wanted us to work things out. I told him I was going through with the divorce and was willing to work out the settlement with him, but at this point, that was all I was willing to do. He asked if there was any possibility we could get back together. I told him I did not know, but if he fought me on the divorce, there definitely would not be. As a result, we worked out a settlement and child support arrangements in a fairly decent manner. The divorce was final a couple of months later in 1973.

I found another job as a waitress and my now ex-mother-in-law stayed with me often to watch the kids while I was at work. I had been awarded the house and quite a lot of child support. I chose not to go on welfare. We were doing okay and had everything we needed. Mostly, I did not want my children growing up with the stigma of being on welfare.

I discovered Eddie was stealing from a store! When I found

what he had taken, I took him and the goods to the store and had him return all of it. Unfortunately, the store did nothing other than to tell him not to do it again. Then he started stealing money from me. One day, after I yelled at him for something he had done, he told me he decided to pack his clothes and run away to his aunt's house. I explained to him that bad things can happen to children who run away. Someone could pick him up on the road, take him, and never bring him back. He said he was going anyway. At that point, Marie decided to go with him. She was already such a caretaker that I believe she wanted to go just to be able to look out for her brother. He was eight and she was six. They packed their bags and left. I waited at home long enough for them to be almost at the highway. I went to pick them up and told them I wanted to take them somewhere to talk to someone. I took them to the police station. An officer spent an hour talking to them. He showed them pictures of lost children, abducted children, and children found dead. Then he showed them the jail and locked them up, pushing me out toward his office. It took my daughter about a minute to start to cry but my son was trying to be a tough guy. After five minutes, he asked to be let out and began to cry. Marie never tried to run away from home again, but Eddie was a different story.

Later that year, my ex-father-in-law offered me five hundred dollars to take back his son. I had heard a lot of things in my life, but this was the most disgusting. If my ex-husband was raised with those kinds of values, I could begin to understand why he was the way he was. Of course I told him no. As a matter of fact, I told him there was not enough money anywhere to make me take him back.

Working and trying to raise my three children by myself

was not an easy thing to do. I decided to rent out one of our spare rooms to a young lady with the understanding that she needed to baby-sit for me while I was at work. That made it much easier.

27 Our Trip to Germany

Oma died on October 1, 1972. In the fall of 1973, Opa wrote and asked if the kids and I could come to see him in the spring of 1974. He would pay our way. I told him we could. My mother had already gone over to be with Opa and she was taking care of the cleaning and cooking for him. In January, 1974, I found a good daytime job with a private employment agency. I was their Administrative Assistant and ran the part-time employment division. I also did their outside public relations work, talking to companies who would use our part-time employment people. They had hired me despite the fact that I would be gone to Germany for six weeks starting in May. With my salary and the child support, the children and I made it just fine and I did not have to worry about losing our house. The divorce had been hard enough on the kids so I did not want to take them away from their friends and school. Unknown to me at the time, my wonderful job would come to an abrupt end in the fall when the owner filed bankruptcy.

In May of 1974, I took my three children to Germany. Eddie was nine, Marie was seven, and Michelle was not quite two. I had not seen Opa in eighteen years and I was very excited about my children meeting their great-grandfather. I worried about communicating with him though–my German was terrible. I had not spoken German for fifteen years and

Opa spoke no English. When we got off the plane in Bielefeld, Germany, I looked frantically to find him. I saw my mother first and then I saw Opa. I was shocked to see that my grandfather was smaller than me. I had this urge to lower myself so I would be smaller than him. I felt almost embarrassed to have grown so much, and I was only five feet tall. I remembered Opa through my eyes as a child when he had been a giant to me in so many ways. As a child, I looked up to him not only in admiration, but also in stature. The physical reality was that my grandfather was four feet eleven inches tall. I reached out, grabbed him, and hugged him. I could hardly believe I was really with him again. I had not seen my mother for over a year and was equally happy to be with her. We had so much to talk about.

Opa loved children and my children took to him as if they had always known him. They could not speak any German, but they managed to communicate just fine with our translations and by signing with their hands. Opa and Michelle were inseparable. I remembered enough German to do fine. Trying to speak it was hard for the first week, but after that it became easier with each day. We spent most of the six weeks with Opa in his small apartment in Marienfeld. It seemed like nothing had changed. It truly was like going home again. Even the furniture in the living room was in the same place. The outhouse was still being used and my children thought that was great. We bathed in the same metal bathtub in the washhouse that I had bathed in as a child. Opa still had the same coal stove in the apartment. The only things different were a washing machine and a small ice box in the kitchen, and a television in the dining area. Opa was older but his spirit was the same. He still liked his coffee time, and he could still talk forever. He smiled and laughed a lot and loved having his family around him. He still sang wonderfully with his whole heart and soul.

It rained most of the time we were there but it made no difference. Opa kept the children entertained. He played card games, board games, and dice with them. Even as small as the apartment was, we never felt closed in. My children got along with each other and they and I had a wonderful time. On nice days, they played in the creek behind the apartment building. We walked to town for groceries every day. The people in town remembered me and it was good to see them again.

Two of my great-aunts and my Godmother lived in the three other apartments in Opa's building. I was able to spend time with them and my children were fortunate enough to get to know them also. One of them raised rabbits and she let the kids feed them. Opa's sister, who lived in East Germany, was allowed to come and visit with us for a couple of weeks. She was a quiet and soft-spoken woman. Her life in East Germany sounded terribly difficult and oppressive. One day she was darning a pair of nylons. I could not believe it and asked her why. She said the Government controlled everything in her life, right down to how many pairs of nylons she could have in a year's time. Everything she and her family needed to live was rationed and people did what they had to do in order to have what they needed to survive. Our family periodically sent care packages to her. She said the government personnel sometimes opened them before she saw them and took out what they wanted, then gave her the rest. I hated to see her go back. No one should have to live under such oppression and deprivation.

I had the opportunity to spend time with my cousins. I went shopping in the next town, called Gütersloh, with one of my cousins. I was amazed at how Americanized everything was. Billboard advertisements of American products were everywhere. Store salespeople spoke English. American products were available in all the stores. My other cousin and his girlfriend took me to a nightclub in another town one evening. I was surprised how plush the club was. It had chandeliers, overstuffed leather furniture, and beautiful hand-cut glass. My cousin told me all the clubs were like that. I controlled my drinking that night because it was terribly expensive and I did not want to become an embarrassment to them. My cousin had only one drink all night long and I asked him why. He said that if he drank more than one drink and was stopped by the police, his license and his car would be confiscated on the spot for a year. Any more than one drink would register too high on a breathalizer. He could not take the chance.

On a warm, sunny day, my mother, cousin, and I took the kids to an outdoor pool in Gütersloh. It was a huge pool area divided into five pools. One had waves like the ocean. Another had every water slide you could want. The third was like a regular pool, the fourth was a diving pool, and the fifth was a small pool for little kids. My kids had the time of their lives.

Opa took us sight-seeing to a park in Essen called Gruga Gardens. My mother, my uncle and his wife, my cousin and her husband went along. The park was absolutely phenomenal. At the entrance, there was a big dolphin pool where we could get close enough to pet the dolphins. We walked into a castle that had been turned into a restaurant and museum. From one balcony, we looked out over almost all of the park. It was a profusion of color everywhere one looked. The trees and flowers were in full bloom. We walked the paths through the park and at every turn there was something for the kids to see or do. There were houses with life-size figures depicting famous fairy tales set up all along the paths. One could push a button and the whole scene would come alive as the fairy tale was told. There was a small, shallow man-made lake with a huge log across one part of it which the kids could walk across, and little boats the kids could take out on the water. Adults were not allowed on this lake.

We spent a few days each at both the home of my aunt, and then my uncle. They lived in different cities. While we were at my uncle's home, they tried to convince me to stay in Germany with the children instead of returning to America. They had a job for me and a place to live if I would stay. It was very tempting because it meant I could leave behind all my problems in the United States and start over. It also meant I would not have to deal with my ex-husband but I knew I would be running away. I decided it would be too hard on the children and I was spoiled by all the conveniences I had in the United States such as the nice appliances, hot running water, my home, and most importantly, the friendly American people.

While visiting my uncle, I went to see my old school friend, Monika. I tracked her down by going to the apartment where she used to live–her parents still lived there. They recognized me and had their son call Monika to tell her I was there. Not only did I get to see her, but she rounded up many of my old schoolmates and we all went out to lunch together. They remembered all that we did together as children–they even remembered my birthday. I was stunned and felt ashamed of how little I remembered about them.

The day our vacation came to a close, we were all very sad. When I said good-bye to my grandfather, we both cried. I had not seen Opa cry before and it made it much harder to leave. I told him I would come back again. He looked at me and said he would not see me again. He was right. Opa vowed he was going to be the first one in his family to live to be eighty years old. In 1979, he had a severe stroke which left him completely helpless and in the hospital. I wanted to go see him but could not. Three months later, one hour after his eightieth birthday, he died.

28 Abandonment

During the summer of 1974, my ex-husband, the children, and I started to spend some time together. Each time we did, we had a wonderful time. He was very kind and sweet to me and treated me with caring and respect. I kept thinking that he and I got along well when we did not live together and I could not understand why we did not get along when we did live together. Anyway, I bought it hook, line, and sinker once again. We were remarried in late December of 1974. We had been divorced for a year and a half, and I really believed we had both changed and our life would be different from now on.

Our life together was different and I was genuinely happy. We rarely argued about anything. We did most everything together and I fell madly in love with him all over again. We wanted another child and three months after our remarriage, I was pregnant. I had a difficult time hanging on to the pregnancy so I spent a lot of time on bed rest. My husband was very supportive, loving, and helpful. His mother often stayed with us to help out. The kids were happier and did better all around. When it came close to the time the baby was to be born, we all sat around the table and talked about names and Michelle came up with a name we all liked.

Elizabeth was born November 9, 1975. My husband stayed with me throughout the entire labor for the first time which pleased me very much. Our life continued to go very well as far as I was concerned. I believed we had both finally grown up and learned how to really care about each other and our children. I did daycare in our home for three children so I could be home for my children. I enjoyed the children and my time at home. I had all the patience in the world taking care of other people's kids. I felt I was helping out financially, and had the best of both worlds.

A year after Elizabeth was born, we decided we did not want to have any more children. My husband did not want to have a vasectomy so I decided I would have a tubal ligation. I had been on birth control for many years and the doctor no longer thought it wise for me to continue on the pills. I tried other alternatives and none of them worked out well for me, so I made an appointment for the surgery. When we were at the hospital and my husband learned that he had to sign a consent form, he hesitated. I asked him what was wrong but he did not share with me what was troubling him. He signed the consent form and I had the surgery believing I was doing the right thing for our family and our relationship.

My husband and I periodically went out together with people from his work. On New Year's Eve of 1975, we hosted a party in our home for all our friends. One of the couples got into an argument and my husband drove the woman home because her husband left without her This same couple hosted a New Year's Eve party at their home the following year. We went and I thought we were having a wonderful time until my husband got so drunk he stayed overnight at the host's house. After that night, we continued going out with this couple as we had been doing. I noticed that my husband spent a lot of time with this woman, even when we were all together. They would go to the jukebox and stand there talking together for very long periods of time. Then they would suddenly disappear for a while and when they returned, they said they had gone outside to talk. I did not want to believe that anything was going on between them so I chose to ignore it.

In April of 1977, the husband of this couple came to my home. He needed to talk to me. He looked as if something awful had happened. I thought something had happened to my husband at work. He said no, but he had something he needed to tell me. We sat down at the dining room table and he proceeded to tell me he found out his wife was having an affair with my husband. He said the affair began before my husband and I remarried and had continued throughout our marriage. He was sorry that he was the one to tell me, but he knew my husband wouldn't and he felt I should know. We talked for a long time because I wanted to know everything he knew before I confronted my husband. I did not want to believe any of this unless my husband confirmed it. You see, over the past year and a half, I had chosen to trust my husband implicitly. Things between us were good and I was content with the way our life had been going. I did not want it to end. When my husband came home that evening, I sat him down and told him his friend had come to see me and told me about the affair with his wife. I asked him if it was true and he told me it was. He said he loved both of us and could not choose between us so he decided to continue the affair after we were married. I was devastated. I stopped doing daycare because of the emotional state I was in. I knew I could not do anyone any good at this time. After a few weeks of emotionally falling apart and reading every self-help book I could get my hands on, I asked my husband what he decided to do about this other woman. He told me again that he loved us both and asked me to stay with him. I told him that since he was unable to make a decision and a commitment, I would do it for him. I filed for divorce and knew I would not allow myself to be manipulated by this man again. I did and said whatever it took for him to give me what I wanted in the divorce. We had what is laughingly called an amiable divorce. It was final in August of 1977.

After the divorce was final, I drowned my sorrows in alcohol. I was a good mother, I thought. I didn't drink during the day because my kids needed me and I did not want them to see me drink. I put them to bed at eight o'clock every night and then I went down in my basement and drank. When I could, I went out to the bars. I did not have to spend any money on my drinking in the bars–all I needed to do was flirt with men and they bought me all the drinks I could take. I drank every night and I consciously drank to achieve a blackout. That was my escape; I wanted to feel nothing. It was to be my last escape.

I was being very hard on my kids and did not realize it at the time. I was so busy feeling sorry for myself and being so self-centered that I did not notice what they were going through. I distanced myself from them emotionally and functioned on a mechanical level in taking care of them. The children, for all practical purposes, had lost their father because he did not see them as often as he was supposed to. Now they had lost their mother as well, to alcohol. Even though I was there physically, emotionally I had abandoned them.

Without realizing it, I made my two oldest children responsible for the two youngest ones. They did all of the babysitting for me so I could selfishly go out when I wanted. There were a few times when I needed to hire a sitter because both of the older children had things going on in school or with church. I hired a young boy from a family I knew to do the sitting for my two youngest children at those times. After three months of having him sit, Michelle, who was now five, had a crying fit one night when I told her he was going to be babysitting. She had not reacted that way before, or toward anyone else. I asked her why she did not want him to come, but she would not say. Thank God I had enough presence of mind to pay attention to her reaction. A half an hour after I had left, I came back, and snuck into the house. The sitter had Elizabeth, who was two, on the living room floor lying on her back between his legs, tickling her in a way that did not look totally innocent. She was not laughing or giggling, instead, she seemed apprehensive. When she saw me, she did not say a word which was strange because whenever I came home after being gone, she always ran to me to give me a hug. I asked him what he was doing. He turned around, shocked that I was standing there, and said, "Nothing." His face turned beet red. Michelle heard my voice. She was upstairs by herself. She started to cry and asked if she could come down. She was scared. It was odd that she would ask such a thing in the first place. I asked the sitter why she was upstairs alone and afraid to come down. He said he didn't know. My stomach told me that all was not right. I had my suspicions, but could not prove anything without one of the kids telling me what was going on. I told the boy he was permanently done baby-sitting for my children. I questioned my five-year-old many times about what the sitter did that made her so afraid, but she did not want to tell me. She began to wet the bed at night and had terrible nightmares every night. I would go up to her room three or four times a night to hold and rock her until she settled down. I took her to the doctor but he found nothing physically wrong. He attributed her behavior to the divorce. He did put her on medication, however, which she took at night before she went to bed to help her not wet the bed. It did not work all the time, but it helped.

God was no longer important in my life. I believed He had abandoned me. In fact, I did not think about Him other than to yell at Him.

I realized that my husband took away my right to have any more children by not being honest with me about his affair. Had I known, I certainly would not have had a tubal ligation. The reason he did not want to sign the consent form in the hospital the day of my surgery was because he knew I would not have had it done had I known. This was one more thing about which I could feel sorry for myself. For the next two years, I toyed with my ex-husband's hopes and affections. He was in and out of my life and my home. I had no feelings left for him but I used him to get what I wanted when I wanted it.

That year, I started to think about my old boyfriend, David. I contacted someone from my hometown and asked about him. He was divorced. I asked the person to find out if he would be willing to meet with me. She called me back a couple of days later. He wanted to see me and would meet me at our hometown bar the following Saturday night. I drove to my hometown and met him. I hardly recognized him. We drove to the town he lived in and he took me around to meet his friends. All of his friends were sitting in bars. Even though I did not recognize my own alcoholism at the time, I did not appreciate him taking me to nothing but bars, and I knew I should not get involved with him again. By midnight the weather turned bad so I headed home. I drove eighty and ninety miles an hour through blizzard conditions on a country road. I was very intoxicated. I outran the police that night and made it to my favorite bar before it closed.

I had taken ceramic classes for many years and my teacher told me that I was so good at it she thought I should start my own business. I thought it was a good idea because I could then stay home with my children instead of having to work outside the home. I borrowed some money from my mother to remodel my basement into a shop and buy a kiln, paint, and other equipment I needed. In the fall, I started teaching my own classes twice a week in the evenings. On the nights I held classes, I sat down to drink as soon as they were over. I wanted to pay my mother back everything I borrowed from her in record time. My business went so well I was able to pay her back six months after I had started the classes.

29 A Hint of Sanity

In early 1978, I found a job at a printing company as a proofreader. I also continued my ceramic business at home.

By April of 1978, my behavior toward the children bothered me. My behavior when I went out drinking bothered me also. I had been involved in one-night-stands, which were totally against everything I believed in. It dawned on me that my behavior might be related to my drinking. By this time I could no longer hold a cup of coffee with one hand because I would shake too badly. I thought it was from stress. Every morning when I woke up, my face, hands, and feet were bloated. I went to the doctor to find out what was wrong with me, but he didn't know. Of course, the subject of drinking never came up.

In May, I was stopped by a police officer at two o'clock in the morning for drag racing down Madison Avenue hill. He asked me to get out of my car and go sit in his squad car. I was so drunk I could hardly talk, much less walk straight. After I made it into the squad car, he said he noticed I had been drinking. I told him I had had a couple of drinks. He laughed and said they must have been very large drinks. He asked if I had kids and I told him yes and that they were home alone. He then asked if I thought I could make it home okay if he let me go with just a warning this time. Of course, I told him I could and that I would drive slowly. He should have thrown the book at me and I was grateful he let me go.

Two weeks later, I drove home in a blackout. In the morning, I heard on the radio that a man was struck and killed on the corner of Belgrade and Center Street in North Mankato at about one-thirty in the morning. The car was described as a small red car. Panic gripped every fiber of my being. After I composed myself a little, I went out to check my car for any dents or signs I may have hit someone. My car was clean! I still wondered if I could possibly have hit that man. For the next week I did not drink. I kept listening to the news to see if they found the person and the car. Finally one day they announced that the driver and car were found! Relief is hardly an appropriate description of how I felt. I went back to my drinking. Two weeks later, I was in a bar drinking when a guy I could not stand asked me to go home with him and I told him I would follow him to his place in my car. As I left the bar, I suddenly felt stark sober. What had I become? How could I even consider going home with this guy? I turned my car around and went home.

The next morning, June 20, 1978, I went to the home of my girlfriend, Ann, for coffee. She was having a terrible time with her husband. He was drinking and quite often became violent. She had joined a twelve-step program to help her deal with the things going on in her life. I had been going over to her house with my children for years. In the past six months, I had listened to the things she said about her program. It amazed me how calm she was about the things happening in her life. She was actually able to laugh about her husband's behavior. I admired how she dealt with her children. When they acted like little brats, she laughed and said they were just being kids. She once told me that as long as the kids did not hurt themselves or others, the world would not come to an end because of what they were doing. So why get all bent out of shape? I liked being around her because of her attitudes about many things and I learned a lot from her. On this particular day, I told her about how much I had been drinking over the past nine months. Since she had not seen me drink or under the influence, she was very surprised. I told her that I did not know what to do anymore. I had tried to quit about a month earlier and just could not do it. I confided to her that I had been doing things I would not have believed I could do, and felt very ashamed of myself. Most of the time, I felt as though I was losing my mind. If I did not get my act together, I was afraid I would lose my children. My son and oldest daughter had already told me they wanted to go live with their father. She said she would ask her husband if he would take me to an Alcoholics Anonymous meeting that night–if I was willing to go. She thought I could get some help there. Her husband had been involved in the program for quite some time, but was using again at the present time. Nevertheless, he took me to my first meeting that night. I did not know it then, but I had found the one thing which would completely change my life!

Chapter 6 - A New Beginning

30 God's Grace

God touched me many times during the course of my life. I always turned away from Him after a short time. Now He was throwing me a lifeline, and it was up to me to grab hold. My first meeting left me full of hope. I came away from there believing there was something I could do about my drinking, myself, and my life. I was not crazy–the problem had been alcohol. I went into the meeting thinking I was truly insane and I came out believing that I was not. That was an absolute miracle to me.

I went to a meeting every night for the next six weeks. I started to feel better physically. A month after I started going to the meetings, I noticed that the shaking I had experienced during the past nine months was gone. I lost all of my friends I had been with over the past twelve years except for Ann. I did not know why, and it was a very painful and lonely experience.

The first weekend of August, my ex-husband and I took our children to an all-day softball game and picnic with some of our mutual friends from the bars. They drank all day long and that night we went to one of their homes to continue the party. I felt really proud of myself because I had not touched any alcohol all day. It was the first time I had been around it in six weeks. These people told me that I did not have a problem and it was exactly what I wanted to hear. My ex-husband took the kids home at about ten-thirty that night to put them to bed and I stayed at the party. By eleven o'clock, I decided since I had done so well all day, I could handle one drink! I staggered home at two o'clock in the morning and actually crawled on all fours for the last half block. I spent the night on my bathroom floor. The next night, I went back to a meeting because I was now thoroughly convinced I needed to be there. I made a commitment to myself that night to stay with the program no matter how difficult it became. For the next six months, every day was a fight for me to not drink. Sometimes it was all I could do just to get through five minutes at a time. The thought of drinking was with me constantly.

I did fairly well the first six months as far as grasping the principles of the program. There were issues with which I needed to deal that my group decided they could not help me with. My mood swings were severe. My group suggested I go into inpatient treatment. I was scared to go so I used my kids as an excuse to not go. That excuse worked for only so long. One night, one member of my group said he would take care of my kids for the month I would be in treatment, so I had no more excuses. I talked to my employers the next day and told them I had a problem and I needed to go into treatment. They were very interested, encouraged me to go, and even asked if they could come to visit me so they could learn more about this. I agreed. I went home and made arrangements to place the kids with the people with whom I wanted them to be. My son was taken care of by a male friend of mine who was also in the program. Eddie knew and liked him and they stayed in my home for the entire month. Marie stayed with my mother, who lived above Grandma's V Store in lower North Mankato. My friend, Ann, took care of Michelle. All of these places were within walking distance of the school my children attended. Elizabeth was two and stayed with my sister. The following day, the man who had offered to take care of all my children drove me to treatment. This was February of 1979.

I had the impression my mother and sister thought this was just one more harebrained idea of mine. I did not feel they believed I should be going to treatment but, as always, they supported my right to do it and gave me all the help I needed. I was grateful for their support. For the first time, it did not matter to me what they thought about what I was doing. I was on a mission to get well so I could have a better life. I was prepared to go to any length in order to accomplish that.

31 Healing Begins

I did not have trouble opening up and talking about the things I needed to talk about while in treatment. I was there for help and was determined and willing to do whatever it took to get the help I needed. The third day of group, my counselor said he had me figured out. The day before, someone in the group talked about throwing a loaded gun at his wife and telling her that if she hated him so much, she should pull the trigger. My counselor said he was lucky that I was not his wife because he believed I would have pulled the trigger. I was horrified! How could he have thought I could do such a thing! He believed I was so full of rage that I could be capable of such a thing. I had been angry a few times in my life, but never had I thought of killing anyone. Even when my ex-husband beat me, I could not make myself kick him on his sunburned legs in order to get away from him. There were times when things were so bad between us that I wished my ex-husband would get killed in a car accident but I had not thought about physically hurting him myself. I knew what fear and frustration felt like, but I really did not think I was that full of rage. It was the beginning of understanding what was really inside of me.

This was a place where I was given permission to realize and admit my true feelings. It was not easy for me this time to talk about the abuse from my father. I began to feel the rage toward him during the second week in treatment and was very afraid to let any of it show. This time I felt if I started to express that rage, I would need a padded room because I would lose all control. I talked about it in little bits and pieces as I was able to. During the third week, with the help and love of my group, I screamed, yelled, and cried as I told them what was going on inside of me. It was after this session that I felt I could now go on and eventually, with a lot of hard work, my life would be all right. I was told that in order for me to ever be alright, I had to forgive. It was not important what it did for the person I forgave; what was important was what forgiving someone for what they had done to me would do for me. This was a very hard concept for me to swallow. They said I did not need to believe it would help me heal. All that was necessary was that I did it. This was a program of action and I needed to act and let the rewards come. I sat down and wrote my father a letter for the first time in twelve years! I told him where I was and a little of what happened to me over the years. I told him I wanted to establish a relationship with him again, but for now it would have to be only through the mail. I told him that I needed to forgive him for what he had done to me so that I could finally heal. I knew I was not quite ready to totally forgive him, but I was opening the door.

I learned that I possessed many good qualities which I

had not acknowledged. It was difficult for me to believe in those qualities because I felt so much guilt over what I had done in the last couple of years. I was told to give myself affirmations while standing in front of a mirror until I started to believe them. I knew there were a lot of things I did well, but that was not the same as being a good person. I was kicking myself so hard for what I had done that it overshadowed feeling anything good about myself. Part of the treatment was to admit to God, to ourselves, and to another person the exact nature of our wrongs. This was required in order for my treatment to be complete. At the time, I certainly did not recognize the nature of all of my wrongs. The ones which were obvious and in the forefront of my mind were easy for me to admit.

We were also supposed to talk about the good in us during the session with a minister and I had much more trouble doing that. I did the very best I could at the time to clean out the closet of my life. What happened throughout this confession was that it began to bring me back to a belief and a trust in my God. I was not so sure He would forgive me for all I had done, but the hope that He might sprung up in me.

The President and Personnel Director of the printing company I worked for came to my Family Week. Many people in treatment were having problems at their places of employment because of the treatment. Their employers were not at all supportive. I was very fortunate to have the support of my company. When my treatment was completed, our counselor said during the last group session that only ten percent of us would stay sober for a year or more. Statistics had shown that most people who go through treatment return to drinking. I had learned that whenever I was told I could not do something, I was determined to prove that I could; my stubbornness would work to my benefit in this case. I vowed to myself that I would be one of the ten percent!

I did not want to leave this safe haven of treatment. I received understanding and nurturing here. It was far too scary to go back out into the world. To work the program in treatment was one thing, but to work it on the outside was quite another. I had learned many things, such as communicating with my children, that I needed to do differently. I was scared to face my responsibilities, my children and, most of all, myself. I knew the real work was just beginning. My counselor told me that whenever I needed to, I could come and sit in on the group. I could call anytime, day or night, to talk to the staff. I felt more comfortable with that safety net in place.

I was expected to go to aftercare once a week for six weeks. My ex-husband asked if he could go with me. I could hardly believe he wanted to have anything to do with any kind of counseling, but I agreed to let him go with me in hopes he would finally look at himself honestly. In aftercare, I saw my ex-husband's games as clear as glass. He twisted everything that had ever happened between us so that it came out looking as if it was my fault. He took absolutely no responsibility for anything he had done. On the way home from aftercare one night, I told him it was abundantly clear that having any kind of relationship with him was an exercise in futility. I told him I no longer wished to see or be with him. I knew I could not avoid seeing him when he picked up the children for visitation, but otherwise I did not have to deal with him any longer. He was finally a closed chapter in my life. My feelings for him, I thought, were finally gone.

The first couple of weeks at home with my children were

very tense. It was like we were all wondering and waiting for an explosion. Slowly we settled in with some new rules of how we were to treat each other. I sat down with my children and talked to them about some of the things I learned in treatment. I explained to them what I needed to do for myself so I could change and continue to grow. I told them I needed to go to a lot of meetings so I would learn how to be a better mother and a better person, and I asked for their help. I told them we all needed to work together and help each other and everything would be all right. I could tell by the looks on their faces that my children were not buying all of this, but they said they would try to help as much as they could. The trust was not in their faces and I did not blame them.

One Sunday morning on the way to church, Elizabeth pointed into the woods and said, "That's where you used to go when you got drunk, cuz that's where all the drunks live." It had been almost a year since my last drink and I was flabbergasted that she remembered my drinking. She was three years old! It was comical that she thought I had gone into the hills to drink and we all chuckled a little.

The first time I allowed myself to have spontaneous fun with my children was in the beginning of May, 1979. Elizabeth spilled a glass of milk at the dinner table. The children all stiffened, ready to see me get upset. Instead, I sat still for a minute, thinking about what my friend, Ann, would do in this situation, and then I started to play in the milk with my hands. I invited the children to join me. Pretty soon we were all laughing and having a wonderful time. Before this, playing with my children had been regimented, like everything else I did with them. This spontaneity felt wonderful. The next heavy rain we had, I ran outside with the children and played in the flooded street with them. I no longer cared what the neighbors thought. I wanted to have fun with my children and there was no one who could spoil the joy I felt. I was beginning to learn how to let the little girl in me play. It felt strange and foreign at times, and I sometimes caught myself looking over my shoulder to see if anyone was looking at me in disapproval. As soon as I would realize I was doing that, I would adopt an "I don't care who disapproves" attitude and keep on playing.

My friend, Ann, was a very good teacher on how to have fun. We did some pretty crazy things together. One night we decided to walk through one of our friends' homes at midnight. We walked in the front door, said "Hi!" and kept on walking through and out the back door, giggling all the way. Another night, we walked back from having coffee at a restaurant, pretending to be totally drunk, hoping the police would stop and try to pick us up. We were good at acting like a couple of kids and it was just what I needed to do for myself.

32 Living Reality

No matter what we do in life, there are consequences for our actions, good or bad. The sad thing is we very often are not the only ones who pay the consequences for our own behaviors. We drag our children with us and they pay for things which were totally out of their control in the first place. Our families suffer with worry, concern and helplessness, if in no other way. During the nine months of my daily drinking, a lot of things happened to my children that I was unaware of. The full extent of what my children went through was something we all had to face.

After my treatment, I noticed that Marie was not comfortable leaving the house for very long. She had stopped going to Grandma's house overnight quite a while ago. She also no longer stayed overnight at her friends' homes. I began to realize that she had taken over many of my responsibilities while I was drinking, and now she did not trust me to take them back. I sat down with her periodically to let her know that I was the Mom again and would take care of things. She needed to be a twelve-year-old and do the things girls her age do with their friends. It took a long time until I earned back her trust.

Michelle was no longer the happy-go-lucky little girl she had been before she was five. She more often than not was sullen, sad, and seemed to live in fantasy. She was still wetting the bed and her nightmares continued, although she no longer had them every night.

Elizabeth was three and a half years old now. She was a quiet, sweet, little girl, and she was the clown of the family. Whenever things got tense, she would do something to help us all laugh. Her favorite thing was giggling. She had such a contagious little laugh that we couldn't help but to start laughing with her.

Eddie decided he was the man of the house. He treated his sisters, especially Marie, in a very mean manner. He tried to manipulate everyone into doing what he wanted them to do. I learned later just how bad he had gotten where Marie was concerned. For the past year, Eddie had been hard to handle. He constantly got into trouble at home and elsewhere. When he had a good day, it was because he wanted something. He refused to take no for an answer and did as he pleased. He did not care about the consequences because he would not follow them anyway. Sometimes when I walked by my son's bedroom door in the mornings, there was a terrible smell coming from his room. I had no idea what it was. It smelled like his room was full of dirty, sweaty, socks. I spent many days in his room trying to find what caused that smell but I could not locate the source.

I came home from work one day to find Eddie on top of Marie, choking her. I couldn't pull him off of her so I grabbed his hair and pulled him off of her that way. He started to fight me. I got him down on the floor, sat on top of him, pulled my fist back, and was about to hit him when I felt such rage inside of me that I stopped dead in my tracks. I vividly remember thinking that if I threw the first punch, I would not stop. I got up off of him, told him to go to his room and stay there. I ran outside and sobbed.

Eddie's behavior was that of a person who was using alcohol or drugs. He was a very intelligent young man, but his grades in school kept going down and he skipped school now and again. He had been a caring and sensitive person in the past, but I had not seen that in him for a very long time. I went through his room one day specifically looking for drugs or alcohol because the day before he had had another very irrational and violent outburst. By this time, I believed he was using something that made his behavior erratic. I found codeine pills and pills of some unknown type. I called my ex-husband and we confronted Eddie about them. He admitted he was taking the pills and had been smoking marijuana since the age of twelve–he was now fourteen! He looked at his father and said, "You do it all the time, so what's the big deal?" He had taken the pills from his father! I told him I wanted him to go to treatment. My ex-husband decided he should see a psychologist instead. So we took him to a psychologist hand-picked by my ex. This psychologist did not believe that a fourteen-year-old could possibly be addicted to drugs. According to him, he was just experimenting. I should have known that because my ex did not want to look at his own using problems, he would find the one guy in town who did not agree with addiction.

After a short time, when Eddie made no improvement, I arranged for him to be admitted into a three-month juvenile treatment center. He was angry with me and threatened me by backing me up against a wall with his clenched fist ready to hit me. He was screaming that he was not going and I could not make him go. I called for help from Social Services and the police. They told him he could either let me take him to treatment or he would be put there through the court system. He decided to go peaceably.

As soon as my son left for treatment, the girls became visibly more relaxed, especially Marie. She now began to stay overnight at friends' homes and do the normal things girls her age do. She had been scared to death of her brother. She told me he had been beating on her for a couple of years when I was not around. She did not trust him with the little ones because of how he had treated her. I felt guilty that I did not see what had gone on. I knew I could not help her deal with all of this by myself so I asked her if she wanted to go to meetings, too. There were meetings for kids her age who went because they knew people who had problems with alcohol or drugs. Marie said she wanted to go. Michelle decided she also wanted to go. Elizabeth was too young and was quite sad when I told her she could not go until she was a little older.

Our whole family was very involved in Eddie's treatment. We went to see him each weekend and all of us–including my ex–were involved in his Family Week. An awful lot of hurts were brought forth and talked about. Forgiveness began for all of us. I felt really good about my son's progress after six weeks and had high hopes for him. When he was ready to be released, Marie absolutely did not want him to come home. I certainly understood, but I told her that if he ever tried to hurt her again, she should tell me and he would have to go live elsewhere. I thought we should give him a chance after all the hard work he had done in treatment. She did not like it and was really apprehensive but she agreed to give it a try.

During Eddie's treatment, we were taught to use the Awareness Wheel from the book *Alive and Aware*[1] by Sherod Miller, Ph.D., Elam W. Nunnally, Ph.D., and Daniel B. Wackman, Ph.D. to help us better communicate with each other. The steps in using the Awareness Wheel are as follows:

My issue is:

1. Interpretation	I think; My idea is; My concern is; I grieve; etc.
2. Sensory Data	I see; I hear; etc.
3. Feelings	I feel; My feeling is; etc. (sad, mad, glad, hurt, afraid, etc.)
4. Intention	I want; I desire; I need; My wish is; etc.
5. Action Plan	I am going to; I will; I have; etc.

This helps deal with the issues at hand without blaming or accusing the person being confronted. It helps each person own up to his or her own feelings about a particular issue. We used this at home and it helped us get through some pretty tough issues. We also used a formula I had learned to help us be kinder to each other. No one was allowed to verbally put down another person anymore. If anyone slipped up, they had to tell the person they had put down a positive thing about them. These things worked well and we all treated each other with more respect.

About a month after Eddie came home, he began to be very demanding again. When he was told no, he did whatever he wanted to do anyway. He was beginning to behave the same way he had before he went to treatment. He was fifteen and decided he did not need to listen to me any longer. He again became belligerent and physically threatening. He decided to go see a girl he had met in treatment. There was one hitch–she lived in International Falls in northern Minnesota. He asked me if I would drive him up there. I told him no and so he hitchhiked all the way up there. The police caught up with him because a trucker called them after recognizing that Eddie was too young to be out on the road. The police called me and asked me to come and get him. I told them that since he had found his way there, he would have to find his way back. They escorted my son back to Mankato, county by county. I called Social Services and asked them to put him into a foster home as he was not listening to me and I could not handle his behavior anymore. The court ordered that he be placed in a foster home two blocks away from our home.

During that summer, a man tried to assault Marie and a friend of hers in one of our town parks. She came home and told me. I asked her what she had done to get away. She said they pulled away from him and ran home. I called the police and reported what she said.

I heard of a program the county had called Victim's Assistance. It was a counseling program for victims of any kind of violence. I went to talk to them about myself and I also took the girls a couple of times. I wanted them to learn about good and bad touch from someone other than me. They told the girls that when someone hurts or touches you in a way that makes you uncomfortable, you need to tell someone so it can be stopped, especially if someone tells you to not tell anyone about what they did. Marie talked openly after some encouragement. Michelle was six and a half and she sat there with her eyes down the whole time and did not talk. This program helped dispel my belief that I had somehow been to blame for the incest and attempted rape in my life.

As time passed, my daughters brought their friends home more often than ever before. Our house was filled with children of all ages almost every day. Marie also brought kids to me who were having problems at home–anything from fighting with their parents to sexual abuse. I talked to them and got those who needed professional intervention to accept the help. It was a wonderful and satisfying feeling that my daughter trusted me enough to bring these kids to talk to me. Her friends began to call me Mom. What a reward that was!

I was still working full time at the printing company but I had to quit my ceramic business because the children were allergic to the fumes the kiln gave off. I enjoyed teaching ceramics very much. At the spring ceramic show and judging, my students entered their pieces. We entered twenty-four pieces and we walked away with nineteen ribbons and five trophies. I felt really good about our success. If one has to give up something, it is far better to give it up after a success. I had three more months of classes in order to give my students time to finish their projects and then I was done.

I decided I needed some help and extra money. The young lady I rented to right after the divorce stayed for only a few months before she moved on. Now I could rent out two rooms since my son was not living at home. I decided to rent to people who were just coming out of treatment and needed a place for a few months to be able to get on their feet. A young lady moved in who was pregnant and not working at the time. She took care of my children as part of her room and board. The second renter was a young lady from the program who needed a place to live for a short time.

I enrolled in college in the fall of 1979. I wanted to be a Chemical Dependency Counselor. I had done an awful lot of volunteer work at the treatment center over the last few months. I was allowed to counsel on a one-on-one basis with clients, work as a stand-in counselor with groups, chart the progress of the clients, give lectures on a weekly basis, and teach the Awareness Wheel to families. The Chemical Dependency program was in the process of being organized at the college and I was getting in on the ground floor of all of this. I took the classes I was advised to take. I loved being in school again. It was easy for me and my grades were better than I ever hoped they would be.

It seemed as though my life was finally on the right track. The children were happier and more at ease. Marie gave up trying to be Mom to the little ones and we had good communication in our home. I was involved in my son's life as much as I could be. I went to three or four meetings a week and life gradually seemed to get better. I realized I had not thought about drinking in four months—the urge to drink had been taken away!

In all that happened since the divorce in 1977, Elizabeth just seemed to have gotten lost in the shuffle. She was a very quiet little girl and she was perfectly content to play by herself, although she did like having a lot of people around at home. She had friends in the neighborhood and played with them every day. She was so inconspicuous we hardly knew she was around. There were times when she was playing that I watched her very carefully. She took in everything that was going on around her. Sometimes she seemed so sad. When I asked her why, she would tell me that she was not sad, it must just be her face that was sad. It was apparent that she was not going to talk about her feelings. She was four years old and a very introverted little girl. She did not want anyone mad at her. When she did something wrong, she came and told me herself. She would tell me what the consequences were for what she had done, and then, on her own, she would implement the consequences.

Michelle still wet the bed occasionally and had nightmares about twice a week now. Her teacher at school said that she was very hyperactive. She said they found many hyperactive kids to be allergic to certain foods and suggested changing her diet to see if it would help. I was given a list of foods to avoid, so we tried it. Within two weeks, my daughter had settled down to the point of being able to sit still for an hour at a time. She started to do better in school, was calmer at home, and slept better. She would still often get melancholy, which I did not understand. Home had been a safe, loving place for quite some time now. I could no longer believe this was still from the divorce. In 1980, as soon as school was out for the summer, I decided to take her to a psychologist. He decided what she needed was a stable male model in her life—

someone who would be there for her and do fun things with her. My ex-husband had taken very little interest in seeing the kids anymore and the psychologist thought it was affecting her. He said he would spend time with her outside of his office. The first time, he told her they would go to the park. He called to cancel an hour before he was to come. The second time, he said he would take her swimming. He was an hour and a half late. The third time, he said he would take her to the North Mankato Fun Days Parade. He came as the parade was almost over. Then he told her he would take her swimming again. He called two and a half hours after they were supposed to have gone and said he could not make it. So much for a stable male model. I cancelled the sessions. After all of this, Michelle seemed more closed in to herself than ever and developed an "I don't care" attitude about everything. She grew angrier and began to demand a lot of attention from me.

The foster home Eddie was in decided they could no longer handle him so he came home. His staying at home never lasted because he continued to use. Three weeks later, I caught him using again so he went to another foster home. I kept regular contact with him but we were not in any counseling together. He liked this new foster home very much. He decided he wanted to stay in the new foster home until he graduated. It tore my heart out and I felt like I had lost my son forever.

One of the greatest gifts I was given in the program at this time was a poem written by Kahlil Gibran in *The Prophet* [2]:

Your children are not your children.
They are the sons and daughters of Life's longing for itself.
They come through you but not from you,
and though they are with you, yet they belong not to you.

You may give them your love but not your thoughts,
for they have their own thoughts.
You may house their bodies but not their souls,
for their souls dwell in the house of tomorrow, which you
 cannot visit, not even in your dreams.
You may strive to be like them, but seek not to make them
 like you.
For life goes not backward nor tarries with yesterday.

I read this over and over again until I realized I had treated my children as possessions, just as I had been treated growing up. This poem helped me to change my attitude and begin to treat my children as precious charges with which I had been entrusted.

33 My Arrogance

During the summer of 1980, I met a man who fascinated me. He was full of energy and very personable. He loved having a good time and each day he suggested something fun we could all do together. He was the father of two boys who lived with him. All of our kids got along fairly well and there were no major problems between them. I had known him only a short while when he started to talk about marriage. I told him I did not believe I was in love with him and it was too soon. He then used the rational approach–I needed a father figure for my children and he needed a mother for his. He would take care of us financially so I could stay home. Since we were being honest and walking into this with our eyes wide open, he thought it would work. We did like each other, the kids got along and, who knew, we could fall in love.

People who were close to me saw things in him which I did not see. They tried to warn me. One of my friends had known him for a number of years. She told me a few things she knew about him. His ex-wife called me and told me things I should have listened to, but he convinced me she only wanted to cause trouble. My biggest problem in all of this was that I had become arrogant. I thought because I had learned so much in the program, I could no longer be conned. I believed this man was sincere in what he said and I thought he was the fun-loving person he portrayed himself to be. I was about to learn a fast lesson about arrogance.

My renters moved out at the end of July because we would be getting married in August. In August, at Michelle's eighth birthday party, we announced to the kids we were getting married. Michelle liked this man very much and was happy about the marriage. My other two daughters were not happy but did not let on how they felt at the time. His boys were thrilled.

Things were fine for a couple of months after we were married. Then I noticed that when I went to meetings, he drove by the club to check if I was there. When I went out for coffee with my friends, he drove by the restaurant to see if I was there and who I was with. We no longer did fun things together. Everything had become routine and tense. He yelled at his boys a lot and took them outside to talk to them which I thought was strange. I never knew why they were being yelled at because they were very good boys. My girls no longer liked it when I went to my meetings, but when I asked the kids what was going on when I was not at home, no one said anything. They were, however, all agitated and I could tell there was fear involved. I asked my husband to tell me what was going on, but according to him, everything was fine.

After Christmas, something happened which frightened me. I was coming up the basement stairs with a load of laundry, and my husband was standing at the top of the stairs. He put his foot in front of my face as if he was going to use it to shove me down the stairs. I looked at him and angrily demanded that he stop that kind of behavior. I realized then that this man had a mean streak in him and I wanted nothing more to do with him. I sat Marie down and privately asked her how he treated them when I was not at home. She broke down and told me that he physically pushed them away from him even when I was at home as long as I was not in the room to see it. When I was gone, he yelled at them, ignored them, or made them go to their rooms so he did not have to deal with them at all.

I confronted him with what I knew, how I felt, and what it was doing to everyone in our home. I told him I was not about to live this way and would be getting our marriage annulled. I gave him one week to get out. The next day he left and the boys stayed with us until he could get a place set up for them. A couple of days later, Social Services called me and asked if I would be willing to have the boys live with me as they preferred to stay with us. Social Services knew me quite well by this time because I worked with them concerning Eddie's placements. It was a pleasant surprise to know they had faith enough in me to be able to care for these children. As soon as the boys' father was told they wanted to live with me, he moved into a different county and came to pick up the boys. There was nothing my county or I could do about it at the time.

By the second week of January, 1981, everything, including the marriage, was legally over. The breakup of this marriage took a terrible toll on Michelle. All the kids had been emotionally hurt. Marie and Elizabeth bounced back from it quickly and quite well. Michelle became angrier and she trusted no one. Since my divorce from her father, I had been involved with a number of men. I brought several of them home to meet my kids. About the time the kids felt attached to them, the relationships ended. I did not realize what a horrendous impact this had on my children, especially Michelle. Now she asked me not to go out with men anymore.

In the twelve-step program I belonged to, I heard many times that we should not get involved in a serious relationship for at least the first two years of sobriety, unless, of course, we were already in one at the start of our sobriety. The reason was so we could concentrate on getting to know the program and ourselves. We needed to learn about our thought processes, spirituality, and emotions. We needed to learn how to set boundaries in our relationships and we could not do that unless we really understood what we wanted in our lives. I had not listened to this suggestion. Now I was ready to do what I needed to do. I made a commitment to myself–I would take two years and delve into myself to gain a conscious knowledge of how I arrive at the decisions I make, and to determine exactly what direction I wanted to take with my life.

34 He Sent an Angel

During the spring of 1981, I was in the process of finding a job. I wanted something that would afford me the luxury of being home with my children as much as possible. That meant I needed an evening or night job. I again needed someone to live in my home who would be willing to baby-sit in exchange for part of their rent.

Sharon must have been specially ordered just for us. She was a graduate student at Mankato State University. She grew up in a large family, loved children, and was a very calm individual. We all took to her right away. There wasn't anything about her to not like. She agreed to move in.

The local state hospital employees were going to go on strike. No one knew for how long, but it looked like it might be a long haul. I applied to fill in if the strike went forward. I was accepted and trained. I would be working twelve-hour shifts, seven days in a row, with one day off in between, for as long as the strike continued. I knew many people who were working there and would lose some of those friendships because of what I was doing. However, I needed to meet my financial responsibilities, and furthermore, I did not personally agree with the strike. The wages and benefits the employees were getting were more than most people ever hoped to make. Yet, they wanted more. They wanted better insurance benefits while I sat with none at all.

Once the strike began, I worked with the severely mentally retarded. I liked the job from the minute I started taking care of the patients. I commuted back and forth to work for about a week. Then things started getting rough at the picket line. It began getting scary crossing the picket line even though I knew almost everyone there. I could not believe these people I had known for years could be so mean and vicious. The hospital brought in a group of very big, tough-looking guys from the Cities to help hold down the violence and protect those of us who were working. Sharon suggested I stay on the hospital grounds for the duration and said she would take care of everything at home. The kids did not like the idea, but as long as Sharon agreed to be with them and I came home on my days off, they agreed. The strike lasted just under three weeks. I made enough money to pay off most of my debts. I only had one big bill left which was on a credit card.

When that job was over, I went back to the printing company I had worked at before. I worked part-time in the mornings and I went back to school. I took one class during the day, twice a week, and one at night, once a week. By summer, I could work full-time. I did not want to work full-time during the day, however, because I wanted to be with my children. We all discussed my finding a night job. Sharon saw no problem with it since she would be there with the children at night. I applied at a truck stop right outside of town and got the job. I was to work eleven p.m. to seven a.m. I intended to quit my part-time job as soon as the credit card was paid off. I was home from noon until ten thirty p.m. every day. On the average, I slept four to six hours a day. It was a hectic schedule, but we managed. Sharon took care of whatever needed to be done that I had not gotten to. We all worked well together and Michelle was doing well. She was not so angry anymore. She only occasionally had nightmares and the bed wetting had stopped.

On my days off, I did fun things with my children like roller skating, playing cards or board games, and we went to the parks. I took them to open meetings at the club. At one of those meetings, Michelle looked around at all the people she knew and commented that we were a part of a very big family. It was wonderful that she felt that way. For a long time now, people from the club stopped at our house every day to visit. Everywhere we went, we bumped into someone we all knew. My children enjoyed knowing so many people on a personal level. They were liked by everyone we knew. When we needed help, it was always freely given.

While Eddie was in his second foster home, I met with him and the foster parents once or twice a month to talk about his progress and about which issues I believed he needed to work on, such as abandonment and his anger with me and his father. I was willing to go to counseling with him, but it was not set up. In the summer of 1981, my son's foster father told me that they could no longer have him stay with them. Eddie was not willing to do the things he needed to, and the foster family was finding it harder all the time to deal with his behavior. He told me I had been right all along concerning the things my son needed to deal with and he was sorry they had not listened. Eddie was stealing and he was using drugs again. He had been caught a number of times and Social Services recommended he be placed into the Sheriff's Boys Ranch in Austin, Minnesota, until he graduated from high school. He was seventeen and would graduate in the coming spring. In court, Eddie's father was asked if he would be willing to have his son live with him and he said no. I could see my son's devastation and anger. Over the past couple of years, his father had had very little contact with him and it hurt Eddie terribly. The court ordered my son to the ranch for six months to a year. During that period of time, I went to see him as often as I possibly could and did whatever I could to see to it he received the help he needed. His counselor was easy to talk with and seemed genuinely interested in what I had to say. He got my son into counseling concerning anger and abandonment. They only scratched the surface, however, because by this time Eddie did not willingly deal with these issues.

Elizabeth started kindergarten in the fall of 1981. I took her to school after my morning job and was able to sleep on the days I did not have an afternoon class as I was again taking two college classes. Between my two jobs, visiting my son, trying to do as much as I could with my children at home, college, and my meetings, my body gave out. Sharon did all she could to help out, but I had taken on far too much. In late October, I was admitted to the hospital with pleurisy and blood clots in my lungs. I was in the hospital for almost three weeks and when I was released, I was told to come in twice a week for the next three to six months for blood tests. They put me on Coumadin to keep my blood thin. I was grateful I was still working for the printing company because of the insurance I had there. I went back to work at both jobs but did not continue my college education. I had earned forty-six credits and only needed nine more to be certified as a counselor. I decided I would return to school the following year.

In December, the kids and I decided we wanted to have an open house on Christmas Day for the people in the club who had no place to go. We baked cakes, pies, and cookies. There were two special fellows in the club who were both divorced and alone. We asked them to come and help us bake cookies. We served the most unusual cookies that year! We had gotten quite creative while making them. Having people over made our Christmas Day very special. We spent every Christmas Eve with my family since I returned to Minnesota. We used to spend Christmas Day with my ex-husband's parents, but that was no longer the case. So, having open house was not only for others, it helped us get through the holidays as well. We still have it every year–it has become a tradition in our family. It is truly a blessing to us.

35 Rigorous Honesty

In 1981, I had begun in earnest to find out what made me tick. I wanted to know why I did the things I did, felt the feelings I felt and thought the way I thought. I attempted to be brutally honest with myself in order to find the answers. The next couple of years would lend themselves to many insights.

I realized that my pride and old sayings such as, "You made your own bed, now lie in it," were the reasons I worked as hard as I did and refused to accept outside help. I did not have to be working two jobs in order to make it financially. In February of 1982, I quit working for the printing company. After another month at the truck stop, I gave up that job as well. I would now work part-time as a waitress. I knew I could make good money in tips and would have more time for my children and the work I was doing on myself concerning the program.

As I searched my soul and became honest with myself, I admitted that I had been a totally authoritarian parent in the past. I had made my children live by my rules without any room for discussion or compromise. I understood that I had been authoritative with them because of my upbringing. I also understood that I was responsible for my actions toward them and could no longer blame my upbringing. I faced the fact that all the decisions I made from the day I left my parents' home were totally my responsibility. I began to understand they had no control nor could they make me do anything once I left their home. To let go of the belief that I had been a victim in life rather than a player, and therefore responsible for the decisions I made was not an easy thing for me to do. I had spent most of my life blaming others for my actions and reactions, now I had to face the fact that these were my choices. Even falling in love was a conscious choice! I needed to learn to make healthy choices, especially in relationships.

Realizing I believed good things would not last very long, I saw the way I had sabotaged my own happiness. When things went well for a period of time, especially in my marriage to the children's father, I created arguments and unhappiness. I lived in crises all my life and when things were too calm for too long, I felt uncomfortable. I was still finding myself creating a crisis, if in no other way, by getting too involved in too many things and putting responsibilities on the back burner. That, of course, ends up creating a crisis in itself.

I had a very difficult time expressing and recognizing my feelings. I was taught to not express or talk about my feelings. Now I had to label them and own them. The difficulty for me was identifying them. I kept wanting to dismiss having them. The only feelings I recognized were hurt and anger. I soon found that I felt anger only after I felt fear. I began to understand that I had been full of fear most of my life, so I must have also been full of anger. Now when I became angry, I had to stop and consciously determine what feelings had come before the anger so I could honestly take care of those feelings. I had turned my feelings of emotional hurt into self-pity. I slung a huge bag full of self-pity over my shoulder as if it were a prize. In the past, I counted on this bag since people would do things for me because of it. Now I hated any hint of pity. I knew as long as I felt sorry for myself, I could not emotionally grow. I wanted to grow out of my past more than I wanted anything.

I found myself apologizing to my children for the first

time and the world did not end! I learned to not make promises because if something happened and I could not keep the promise, trust was lost. I went to people I had hurt in the past and apologized for my behavior. All of them were very receptive and forgiving. I learned this was only the beginning in the lessons of what self-responsibility really means.

I began to recognize when I tried to create a crisis. I learned to listen to my gut reaction in everything I wanted to do. If my stomach did not feel calm when I chose to do something, then I knew I should not do it. It worked as long as I was willing to listen to it, but there were times my head and my wants got in the way, and when I allow that to happen, it never failed to be the wrong choice for me.

The overriding feeling I still lived with was fear. I had abandonment issues which I had not recognized before. I had financial fears, parenting fears, action and reaction fears, and I now needed to work through them one at a time, as best as I could.

Forgiveness for my father was still at arm's length. He and I were communicating by letter and phone. I realized that the anger I felt for him was very much alive. I knew I had to get rid of it because as long as I carried it, he was still controlling me. I did not know how to get rid of it. Willing myself and praying to forgive him were not working.

There was a couple who helped with a youth group called About Face. This couple was in the psychology field and helped counsel the group. I talked to them about my father. They said they knew of something I could do to get rid of the rage. I met with them once a week for the next six weeks. By the fifth week, they said I was ready to do an exercise which would help me get rid of the rage I still felt. They covered their living room floor with pillows and told me that my father was underneath those pillows. Whatever I decided to do about it was all right. There would be no consequences for my behavior toward him this night. I could say and do whatever I wanted to. I felt very awkward and stupid going into this. They helped me get into doing this by reminding me of the things he had done to me. That night, I spent an hour beating, cussing, crying, and screaming into those pillows until I lay down from exhaustion. They picked me up and cradled me in their arms until the tears stopped. From that night on, I have not felt rage. When the rage was gone, forgiveness began to take its place. I will never forget, but my emotions are no longer tied up in the remembering. It was in this act of letting go that I realized my father finally had no more control over me. It was in the forgiving that I realized God had been with me and now I was no longer angry with Him either. In His love and mercy He guided me to the one thing which I could understand and work in order for my physical, emotional, psychological, and spiritual healing to take place. That was the twelve-step program and the people in it. I began my walk with Him in prayer. My trust in Him would take a little cultivating and in time I would count on Him to be my best friend.

36 Becoming Assertive

In June of 1982, Eddie graduated from high school. He had done well scholastically and was released from the ranch to come home. He stayed home about a month and then moved in with friends.

Sharon graduated from college and also left us during that summer.

My house had two bedrooms in the basement and one extra bedroom on the main floor. I rented out all three by the time fall came. Our home was laughingly called the Half-Way House. The three renters were all males. I was not sure this would work but we were lucky as all three were very nice and easy to get along with. One basically wanted a place to put his clothes and we only saw him once or twice a month. He stayed for a year. Another was a young man who needed some extra help learning how to be self-sufficient and I enjoyed helping him learn how to cook; he stayed for several months and then got a place of his own. The name of the last gentleman to move in was Ben. He was semi-retired and stayed with us for two years. He was a surrogate grandfather for my children. I continued to work because my children were all in school full time, so I worked during their school hours.

I was in the middle of a lawsuit which I had filed in early 1979. A government agency had contacted me in the fall of 1978 and said they wanted to winterize and fix anything weather-related in my house. If I lived in my home for seven years after the work was completed, I would owe nothing. I had no intentions of moving so I decided to have them do the work. I was thrilled because I needed the attic insulated and new storm doors. They completed the work, and as soon as it started to get cold outside, we began to have terrible moisture problems. Everything I had stored in the attic was ruined by water and there was continual dripping inside my walls. I called them back several times but they did nothing to correct the problem. After a few months and no action from them, I decided I had no other recourse but to sue them. I did not have the money to fix what they messed up and it desperately needed to be fixed. In late summer of 1982, we finally went to court. They had tried to negotiate a settlement with me but what they offered me was utterly ridiculous and I was determined to get the total amount needed to fix the damage incurred over the last three years. By this time, the government and three other companies were involved. I was going up against them all. The program taught me that I needed to stand my ground and not let anyone victimize me. If I truly believed I was right about something, I needed to see it through until I felt I had been fairly dealt with. Two minutes before we were to enter the courtroom, they settled for the amount I wanted. The amount I received would be enough to fix everything that needed to be fixed. When it was all done, I had enough money left to pay off my credit card. I promptly cut it up and have not owned one since.

    I had been dating a man from the program for a few months now. I did not allow myself to get emotionally wrapped up in him though. He was nice enough and my children loved him, but I saw things in him that reminded me of the good old days of my past and I wanted none of his controlling and manipulating. We had a wonderful time together as long as we went out as friends. Over time, he became possessive and demanding and I refused to continue to date him, but we did remain friends. I realized I was beginning to set boundaries.

    Eddie was having a tough time and periodically came to me for money. He was still using drugs and alcohol, so I told him he was welcome to eat with us, but that I would no longer give him cash. If he needed food, I would go to the store with him and buy him what he needed. He only stopped by when he wanted something and occasionally he asked if he could move back home. The rule in our home was that anyone who lived in it could not be using. Each time he came home to live, I found out he was still using and I had to tell him to leave. It seemed the more I tried to do for him, the more futile my help became. He was in and out of the program and it seemed he could not decided what he really wanted to do with his life.

I love my mother very much and over the years she had been there for me whenever I needed help of any kind. I became aware, however, that she constantly tried to get me to do what she wanted me to do. If I did not cooperate, she got angry and tried to make me feel guilty. I knew she was not aware she was doing this. When I could not take this anymore, I sat down and wrote her a letter. I told her how I felt and that I would no longer allow her to treat me in that manner because it felt degrading. My mother lived in Mankato at the time and I waited for a response, but it did not come. I did not see or talk to her for almost six months. The silence was broken on Thanksgiving Day when we were both at my sister's home. We avoided each other for about an hour. I finally asked her if she was ever going to speak to me again. We hugged and cried together. We talked about it and our relationship has been better than it ever was before. It is now based on mutual respect of our individualities and life-styles.

I stayed away from my sister as much as I could for a couple of years. In her efforts to help me over the years, she had taken on the role of mothering me. She only wanted to do whatever she could to help, and deep down I knew that. After being in the program for a while, I began to grow up and make changes in my life. Her suggestions and help at the time felt like control and I wanted none of it. In my mind, she did not want to let go of her influence over me. Since I did not know how to tell her this, I stayed away from her. This year I went to see her and was able to tell her how I felt without hurting her. Our relationship began its journey to mutual respect.

My father came to Minnesota to visit for the second time since my sobriety. He lived in Arizona. The first time he came, we visited for about two hours. That was all I could handle at that time. This time when he came, I talked to him about what he had done. He listened, cried, and apologized. I told him that I was able to forgive him, but I could not trust him around my children. Therefore, I would not allow him to stay overnight in my home or be alone with my children at any time. He said he understood and respected my decision. I found out very soon he did not understand the full implication of what he had done nor what I had said. In the spring of 1983, he asked me to send my children down to him for a week of their summer vacation. I reminded him of our conversation and told him absolutely not.

My children had been able to manipulate me quite well since my sobriety. I realized I was not doing myself or them any favors by letting them get by with this. By far, this was the most difficult thing for me to deal with, and, in some respects, I still deal with it today. Since my sobriety, I had not been firm or consistent with the children. All they needed to do was cry, get angry, or wear me down by begging long enough and I gave in to what they wanted. I still felt guilty for what they had gone through during my drinking and I felt bad for them because their father did not see them as often as he was supposed to. I knew I needed to change and be consistent in what I said and did. I began to do just that and had very angry girls on my hands. They still wore me down now and again but by the end of 1982, Marie and Elizabeth were accepting "no" answers pretty well. Michelle had much more trouble with them. She still tried to wear me down on everything. Unfortunately, I gave in to her many times when I should not have. I would pay the price for that in the next few years and so would she.

In the winter of 1982, I took part in a "Beginning Experience" weekend at Good Counsel Academy in Mankato. The weekend was about grieving for our losses and saying goodbye to whatever we needed to let go of. I went because I realized there were things I still hung on to concerning my relationship with my children's father. I knew I could not go on with my life in a healthy way until I let them go. The last day of this weekend, I was finally ready to say good-bye to the emotions of that relationship. When I did, I felt released and free. After that weekend, I no longer felt romantic emotions toward him when I saw him.

1. Sherod Miller, Elam W. Nunnally, Daniel B. Wackman, *Alive and Aware* (Minneapolis: Interpersonal Communication Programs, Inc., 1975) p. 30.
2. Kahlil Gibran, *The Prophet* (New York: Alfred A. Knopf, Inc., 1923) p. 17.

Chapter 7 - Discovering Love

37 A Friend and Partner

I had known this man since early 1979. After my meetings, a few of us would go out for coffee and he was always with us. He was a quiet person with a wonderful sense of humor. He was kind, understanding, a good listener, and he helped anyone who needed help. He did not talk very much, but when he did, it was profound or humorous. I admired him very much. He was one of the men who helped us bake Christmas cookies, came regularly to our home to play cards, and had been there several times for dinners. I enjoyed being around him, but I did not think about dating him. I didn't think he would be interested in someone like me. I was still working at the restaurant and I waited on him quite often in the mornings. In January of 1983, I realized that every time I had gone to the restaurant for the past year, the first person I looked for was this man. I was in love with him! I talked to a couple of my friends about this and they said it was about time I realized my feelings for him! They had known I was in love with him for over a year by my behavior around him and how I talked about him. I began to drop subtle hints to him that I was interested in dating him. A couple of weeks later, when he still had not asked me out, I decided to throw caution to the wind and allow myself to be vulnerable. I made sure I was at the restaurant before anyone else one night so I could talk to him alone. I had to know if there was a chance we could have a relationship. If he said no, I could go on with my life, but not knowing how he felt made me feel like I was dangling in limbo. I slid into the booth next to him and said,

"So, are you ever going to ask me out, or what?" So much for subtlety! He was silent for a few seconds, then looked at me and said, "Sure, when do you want to go?" I invited him to the house after coffee and we played gin rummy for a couple of hours and talked. When he left, he kissed me goodnight. We were together almost every day from then on.

I loved his philosophies of life such as "the only way to acquire patience is to wait for it." He believed the reason many relationships do not work is because of expectations. He felt if he had no expectations of people or situations, he could not be disappointed, and everything that happened could then be a surprise, insight, or adventure. He also believed that all individuals need to retain their own individuality in any relationship and do what is needed for themselves in order to continue their own walk through life. He would say, "There is you, there is me, and then there is us." He believed if we did not take care of ourselves, then we could not take care of a relationship and there could be no "us."

From the very beginning of our relationship, this man took the spiritual lead. We prayed together every day. He made it so matter-of-fact that I was not uncomfortable. A few months after we started dating, he and I discussed his moving into my home–we were together every day anyway. In May, my friend moved into our home. Once a week, we invited people over to play Uno. There was a lot of laughter in our home. He liked doing things spontaneously. I had not been able to be spontaneous and feel comfortable doing so more than a few times in my life. He made it so easy for me to drop what I was doing and go do something fun, even if it was just to feed the ducks at Spring Lake Park. He involved himself with the children as much as they allowed him to and was very sensitive to their feelings. He did not force himself or the things he wanted us to do together on them.

My friend had a camper and we went camping every weekend we could during this summer. The children loved it and so did I. He also worked in building construction and had his own remodeling business. He took small jobs for private home owners. I liked to paint and we talked about combining the two and working together. He did not like to paint very much but we began working together that summer on painting houses, apartments, and on small remodeling jobs. Marie also worked with us periodically.

During the summer, my friend told me it had been years since he had seen his mother. I noticed sadness in him when he talked about his family. I wanted to meet his family, which consisted of his mother and twelve brothers and sisters. We went to see his mother and she was a warm, outgoing, loving, and funny lady. I liked her right away and the feeling seemed to be mutual. From that first meeting with his mother and some of his brothers and sisters, I have felt as if I was part of his family.

In the middle of July, Marie talked to us and asked us if she could go into treatment. I was stunned. I did not believe she was having a problem with chemicals or alcohol. She proceeded to tell us that when she stayed overnight at certain friends' homes on the weekends, she would get terribly drunk. She said she had done things she was ashamed of and could not seem to get a handle on her using. I still thought she was only experimenting because I saw no personality changes in her. She asked us if going to treatment would hurt her. Of course, we agreed it would not, and told her she could go. My friend went out to the garage and I went with him. I broke down and cried. He put his arms around me and held me until I could quit crying.

After Marie's treatment, she was doing well and grabbed a hold of the program. At home, we supported her in every way we possibly could. My fear was that she would go along the same path her brother had chosen. Each time she went out with her friends, I panicked, afraid she would use again. My friend told me we were doing what we could to put her on the right path but it was up to her to use what she had learned. Other than encouraging her and supporting her in her effort to do that, we could do little else. I knew he was right but it was difficult for me to let go.

By late fall of 1983, Eddie was in and out of jail and was using heavily. One night I received a phone call at two o'clock in the morning. The person at the other end said, "You better be watching your little one when she walks to school. You never know, something could happen to her." The voice on the other end of the phone was my son's. He was obviously high on one of his favorite drugs. I became frightened for my daughter's safety. I had to assume my son could be capable of doing just about anything to anyone if he was high enough. I took my daughter to and from school every day until my son was court-ordered to treatment for the second time shortly thereafter. This time, I refused to have anything to do with his treatment. I had been to three Family Weeks with him and I was not willing to go through another one. I did not want to give up on him, but he had been through his sister's Family Week with us just a short time ago. In his case, the time for discussion was over. It was time for him to act and I was tired of listening to the excuses for his inaction. Shortly after his treatment, he was using again and was very angry with me for not going to his Family Week.

My friend was a fantastic support to me through all of this. He did not try to tell me what to do about anything. He was there for me to lean on and to talk things over with. He was there for my kids and did not shy away from being involved in their treatments or their lives. I often wondered why he stayed around with all these problems going on. He certainly did not need all this in his life. He had raised his two boys. Why should he want to take on helping me raise my children? I had met his two boys and they were wonderful people.

Even by this time in our relationship, my friend and I had not fought, argued, nor exchanged one hurtful or loud word toward each other. This was totally new and amazing to me. We discussed things and came to solutions we could both accept. He was the most patient, understanding, and supportive man I had ever known. We discussed the boundaries in our relationship. We both agreed that returning to the use of alcohol or chemicals was not an option for us because our relationship would not survive. Infidelity would not be tolerated by either of us. He could not live with fighting and arguing. I could not live with being controlled or under any threats, physical or otherwise. He wanted our relationship to be a mutual partnership, where we helped each other wherever needed. We both needed to have the freedom to pursue our own friendships and our own interests without interference from each other. We both agreed to go to counseling together if we reached an impasse in our attempt to solve a problem in our relationship. We made a commitment to treat each other with respect and dignity. We realized we each had our individual needs and wants. We would do all we were able to do to meet each other's needs. Our wants were negotiable. It was of paramount importance to both of us that we accept each other as the individuals we are and not to try to change each other. We needed to encourage and support each other in our individual attempts to grow and change. We agreed to never use our past mistakes and behaviors against each other.

Right before Thanksgiving in 1983, we were blessed with an eighteen-inch snowstorm. Everything came to a standstill for three days. My friend asked me to go for a walk with him after the storm subsided. The streets had not been plowed yet and it was like a fairy tale scene outside. Everything was covered by a sparkling blanket of white. We walked down toward Spring Lake Park. He pulled me under a huge pine tree ladened with snow. He turned to me and asked me to marry him. It took me all of a half-a-second to say yes. Later, he told our friends that if I had said no, he would have pulled one of the branches and no one would have been able to find me until the spring thaw! We decided to get married on our birthdays. We have the same birthdate! It only made sense to make it our anniversary, too.

We celebrated Christmas Eve at my sister's home as usual, except this Christmas seemed more special than most. On Christmas Day, we had our family celebration in the morning. Eddie was to spend the day with us and he came that morning. I am not sure what happened to set him off, but late that morning after the gifts had been opened, he began to yell at me and call me all sorts of names. This kind of behavior was not tolerated in our home. The morning ended by me having to tell him to leave. That was hard for me to do and I felt terrible. Our open house started at three o'clock and I needed to pull myself together before then. I realized I was afraid of Eddie's behavior and I no longer wanted to be around anyone I felt afraid of. I knew there was nothing more I could do to help him except to pray for him, and knowing that hurt. I had lost him after all and I felt an emptiness inside that no one was able to fill. My fiancé tried to assure me I had done what I needed to do and the kids agreed. It did not take away the ache that was in my heart.

After the holidays, we were busy getting ready for the wedding. We included our children in our plans and asked for their input concerning the wedding. As we could afford it, we bought the things for the wedding so by the time the day arrived, everything was paid for. Our children were in the wedding party. Many of our friends offered their help in whatever way they could. It seemed as though our wedding had become a community effort. My fiancé's youngest son, Emery, created the artwork for our invitations and Marie composed the writing on the inside of the invitations. Our wedding party consisted of my fiancé's oldest son, Omar, as groomsman, his friend, Junior, as best man, Marie as bridesmaid and my friend, Louise, was my maid of honor. Michelle was the ring bearer, and Elizabeth was the flower girl. Emery was our photographer since he was studying to be one. Ben gave me away. Our friends from the program were attendants and ushers. Friends helped to make all of the food for the reception and my mother baked a special cake for us. On March 11, 1984, we were married. Our wedding was very special and beautiful. There were about one hundred and fifty friends and relatives who attended. The reception was in the church basement and lasted longer than any I have ever attended. Everyone had a wonderful time and our wedding was so special that people still talked about it two years later. The only sadness that day was that I could not allow Eddie to be at my wedding. He was using heavily and I would not take the chance of him ruining this day for us, but I missed not having him there.

Ben, our renter and friend, still lived with us. He and my husband had gotten along well. They played a lot of cribbage together and were always joking around with each other. After our marriage, we decided we needed more privacy in our home and would try to make it financially without renting out rooms. Ben moved out during that summer. It was hard to see him go since he had been with us for two years.

Marie had done really well with her sobriety. She did well academically and was involved in synchronized swimming in school. A couple of weeks before her graduation, she told us she was going to go to parties her friends were having. She wanted to let us know that she would probably be drinking. There was little we could do except try to talk her out of what she wanted to do. When that did not work, we told her we did not want her to come home after these parties if she was drunk. She agreed to stay at her friends' homes.

Two days before she was to graduate, she decided to move in with people she had met at some of these parties. This kind of impulsive behavior was not at all like her. She had always been very sensible and thought things through before she acted. She was not eighteen yet, but trying to stop her would only have alienated her from us. She and a friend of hers were working for us that summer and she could support herself. On one job, my daughter picked up her sweatshirt and a plastic bag full of a green substance fell out of the pocket. It was marijuana. My husband and I were both very upset. She told us it was not hers; she was holding it for one of her friends. I did not see any signs in her personality that she was using drugs, so I chose to believe her. As a lesson to not keep such things in her possession, she was not allowed to work with us for the next three days. During the course of that summer, I learned she was using drugs and alcohol all the time and I worried about what she was getting herself into. At the end of the summer, she and a boyfriend moved to Spencer, Iowa, because she wanted to go to college there. By this time, I was glad she was moving away because her behavior had become erratic and this way I did not have to watch her go downhill from her use of chemicals. There was nothing I could do for her since she refused to listen to logic and common sense any longer. The boy she moved to Spencer with was also using and I suspected he was beating her, but she denied it. It was difficult for me to understand how my daughter could go from being a very responsible young lady to living the life-style she was now living. I felt helpless and very worried about her.

As soon as Marie and Ben moved out, Michelle started to act out her anger on a daily basis. She demanded all of my attention and if I tried to concentrate on anyone except her, she created such a crisis that I had no choice but to focus my attention back to her. She let it be known she did not like my husband! Yet, if anyone besides herself ever said anything negative about him, she defended him. I could not make sense out of this, it was so bizarre. The way she behaved during the next few years made very little sense to us. There were periods of time when she seemed happy my husband was with us and then, all of a sudden, she would act out again and treat all of us terribly, especially my husband. He had done nothing to cause such behavior from her. On the contrary, he did his best to relate to her and have fun with her. There were times he would wrestle with the girls and it always ended up with Michelle getting angry with him. It seemed nothing he tried to do to help their relationship worked.

Elizabeth was her quiet, sweet self through all of this. She loved to play games, so we sat down and played with her as much as we could. She and my husband grew close and still have a good relationship.

Also during that summer, Eddie had been in jail and treatment. He came over to our house quite often now to visit and for dinners. I did not trust him, however. There had been too many times when I trusted him and he proved himself not worthy of it. He came over to our house one day and ranted and raved at me. My husband, who had not interfered in my relationships with my children before, stopped him in the middle of his yelling and told him he would not tolerate his treatment of me any longer. I had not yet fully grasped the concept of detachment which my program was trying to teach me. At this time, I not only detached myself from my son physically, but I also detached myself emotionally to such an extent that for the next two years I was oblivious to what he did, and treated him as if he were a total stranger. At the time, it was the only way I could emotionally survive.

In the fall of 1984, we had people in our home once a week for our Uno games. The kids could play whenever they chose to. Elizabeth loved to play and joined us quite often. Michelle did not cause problems when we had people in, so I intentionally invited people over as often as possible. We even held some meetings in our home.

This had been quite a beginning for our marriage. Even so, my husband and I grew closer and managed to have fun.

In July of 1985, we took a week's vacation and joined our friends who were going to a National Camping Convention in Grand Island, Nebraska. The campsite was on a huge fair grounds. There were five thousand camping units and over ten thousand people in attendance. The children were bussed to a swimming pool in town a couple of times so they could stay cool, and we had a baby pool at our campsite to dangle our feet into for relief from the heat. At night, they had parades through the camp. The children were a part of them and had a great time. Each day, they had special activities for the adults and children such as live entertainment, games and flea markets. Every evening, several states hosted get-acquainted gatherings. We met people from all over the United States and Canada. Two days before the campout ended, it began to rain. We were lucky we left when we did because the people who left after we did had to be pulled out of the muddy fields. At the campout, there were only very cold, makeshift community showers with no privacy. One had to take showers in one's swimsuit. Despite all of that, it was a new experience and we enjoyed it. Camping had been a Godsend to us every summer because it gave the kids a lot of freedom and it gave my husband and I our own special time together.

In the fall of 1985, Elizabeth asked to take gymnastic lessons, so we enrolled her in classes. She enjoyed it immensely and learned it quickly. She was also doing very well in school. She worked hard at everything and I could see she strived for perfection in all that she did. There were times she would get so upset with herself if she did not catch on to something right away that she would cry out of frustration. As far as I was concerned, she was putting too much pressure on herself. We sat down with her and told her it was wonderful that she wanted to be good at the things she did but it was okay to not be able to do everything perfectly. It was more important that she have fun with what she was doing instead of making work out of it. We both told her that we loved her no matter what her grades were or how she did in gymnastics. She was a caring, loving, and wonderful little girl and that was what really mattered to us. She had always been very self-motivated and even at her current age of ten, she had goals she wanted to reach and did all she had to in order to reach them.

38 Primeval Therapy

In 1986, Eddie was in legal trouble again. This time the judge decided he had been sent to treatment enough times and another treatment would not do him any good. Instead, he strongly suggested to our son that he join the service instead of spending time in jail. Ed joined the Army and after basic training, he came home for a few days. He seemed to be on the way to recovery. His attitude and behavior after basic training took a dramatic turn for the better. I felt hopeful for him and for our relationship for the first time in a long while. It was a relief to have him in the service, because I now knew he was getting three meals a day and had a roof over his head.

I was at the point of counting the days until Michelle graduated from high school and moved out. She was fourteen years old and I was not at all sure I could keep my sanity with her for another four years. Trying to handle her outbursts was overwhelming and emotionally draining. The only thing that sometimes kept me going was the fact that she had not always been this way and I knew somewhere inside that little body of hers was that happy, carefree, loving little girl she used to be. I believed if I hung in there with her, sooner or later I would get her back again.

Marie and her boyfriend moved back to Mankato from Spencer. They were both still using and tried to hide it. We could tell when he was into his heaviest using because during those times he completely stayed away from our family. Marie made all kinds of excuses for him, but we knew what was going on. I spent as much time with her as I could.

During the summer, the girls were old enough to be left alone in the daytime for a few hours at a time, so I worked with my husband as much as I could. Our neighbors told us that they would keep an eye on the kids so they didn't kill each other or burn the house down! They actually did quite well together that summer. I enjoyed working and being with my husband. We worked well together and only occasionally got short with each other when we were tired or hot. Whenever that happened, we would take a break and talk about what was going on with each other. Then things went well again. My husband and I went to a lot of meetings and out for coffee afterward. That gave us time to be with our friends. No matter where we were, however, we would get a phone call from the girls because they were fighting or one of them was asking if they could do some specific thing. Sometimes it was so bad that I had to go home and settle things down.

In the first two years of our marriage, my husband and I occasionally had problems communicating with each other. We were both afraid to confront each other about issues that bothered us because we each though the other might end the marriage. My husband was sometimes too patient for his own good and he minimized his feelings. I let issues build up to the point where I could no longer sleep. Then I did what I called Primeval Therapy. I would get into the car and drive down the road screaming and crying until I had very little energy left. I also went to Seven Mile Creek outside of town and walked into the woods to scream until I could scream no longer. It was a wonderful release for me. I would then go home and be ready for the next onslaught of problems. Sometimes when we had a tough time talking to each other, my husband and I took walks or went to restaurants, and there we were able to talk through our problems. Working through our issues was very painful and painstaking for both of us, but we got through them because we were both willing to compromise. Besides going to meetings and working on our individual programs, we availed ourselves of our minister's counseling during these two years. We also talked with him as a family in trying to help solve some of the problems Michelle was having, and in hope that Elizabeth could talk more about what she was feeling. We had Michelle counsel with him alone, also. We did everything we could to better our family situation and to help our daughters.

During this year, I took the children's father back to court and charged him with neglect of his children's physical safety. He had been involved in a car accident with the children and he had been drinking. Talking to him about it was like talking to a brick wall with an attitude. He only saw the children for a couple of hours a month because that was what he chose to do, yet he refused to abstain from the use of alcohol for those two hours. The judge told my ex-husband that as the children had expressed a desire to see him more often, he hoped to see more of an interest in his children from my ex-husband in the future. He was court-ordered to not use on the day of, and during, visitations. He did not abide by the court order. I instructed the children to refuse to get into the car with him, or anyone else, if they had been drinking. They were to call me and I would pick them up from wherever they were. They did not do that, however, when they were with their father because they were afraid if they said anything to him, he would stop seeing them all together. Even so, they did start calling me to pick them up when they were baby-sitting and the people came home intoxicated.

39 Trip to Florida

In early 1987, we decided to take a trip to Florida. When we told the kids, they could hardly contain their excitement. We flew down there on the seventh of March. We rented a car and had reservations at a motel in Kissimmee, Florida, which is just a few miles from Disney World. When we arrived at our motel, my husband and I wanted to spend the day relaxing and settling in, but the girls, of course, were raring to go, so we went to Old Town which was just a few minutes away. It is a four-block area that was built as an 18th century town. The buildings are the authentic architecture of that time period and they were decorated in the most fantastic colors. There were horse-drawn carriages in which we could ride and each shop was filled with handmade items, and we watched as they were being made. They had shops where they made taffy, chocolate, and all different kinds of candies. We watched a man blow glass into beautiful objects. Each shop and building was unique. At one end of the town, they were in the process of building a huge merry-go-round.

The next day we toured the Kennedy Space Center and saw our first alligator in its natural habitat. There were sea gulls flying all around us waiting to be fed. The girls were feeding them but every time Elizabeth tried to feed them, one would defecate on her. She got so disgusted she cried and wanted nothing more to do with them. We were surprised at how massive the space ships were and could not imagine that they could actually ever leave the earth in flight. When we left the Space Center, we drove along the ocean and stopped at different piers to talk with people. They showed us the fish they had caught. We had not seen those kinds of fish before. They looked weird and had strange names. We drove to a huge beach and went wading in the ocean. We gathered shells we wanted to take home. It was wonderful to see the kids play so freely in the water and on the beach. We walked, explored, and played there for a long time.

On Monday we went to Disney World. We took every tour and ride we could find. Some of the rides seemed to go underground. The displays we rode through were breathtakingly beautiful and very exciting. They had a parade during the day but it was so crowded we could hardly see anything. My husband and I enjoyed that day more than the children did. They were quite disappointed because they had expected it to be much more than it was. They thought it had far too many shops and was too commercialized. We saw everything we wanted to see in a matter of four hours. The girls wanted to go to the Epcott Center, but we were tired! The tour of Epcott took several hours so we let them go in with the tour and we went back to our motel and Old Town to relax until it was time to pick them up.

On Tuesday, I wanted to tour the National Tupperware Headquarters since I was selling their products. The girls did not think that was something they would be at all interested in. They wanted to go to Water Mania. Since it was a warm day, we let them spend the afternoon at the water park while we toured Tupperware.

We went to Sea World on Wednesday. We enjoyed that more than anywhere we had been. We fed and played with the dolphins. There were performing seal, sea lion, and whale shows all day long. They had ponds full of fish waiting to be fed, and beautiful garden paths to walk through wherever you went. There was so much to see and do, we barely accomplished it all that day. We went out to eat at a special seafood restaurant that evening because it was our anniversary and our birthdays! A couple of hours after we were in our motel room that night, Michelle became violently ill. A short time later, my husband and I became ill as well. We called a medical center and were told we probably had food poisoning. We had all eaten the same things, but realized that Elizabeth had not eaten any drawn butter with her meal. She was the only one not sick. The next day, the three of us were so weak that we could not go anywhere. My husband and I spent the day lying around in the room and by the pool while the girls swam.

On Friday we felt better and decided to take the girls to the Gulf of Mexico by Tampa. We spent the day at the beach feeding the gulls, hunting for shells, and exploring. We were amazed that the shells were so different at each beach. We toured some quaint shops we found and looked for souvenirs to bring home.

It was time to go home on Saturday. We had all enjoyed our vacation and the girls were wonderful during the entire trip. There had been very little bickering between them and there was no nastiness during the trip from Michelle.

40 Power Without Responsibilities

We had been home from our Florida trip for not quite a week when Michelle wanted to go to the Cities for the weekend with a neighbor family. I told her I could not afford to pay for her to go. She became very angry and began to yell and cry. I yelled back at her and things escalated into a screaming match. I moved toward her as a physical threat. She then went over to the neighbors and called her father who told her to call Social Services and she did just that. An hour later, I had a police officer and a Social Services Officer at my front door. All Michelle had said to the worker on the phone was that she did not want to live at home any longer. She was sobbing while she was talking to them. They had to assume something awful was going on in her home. She and I then both told them what had really happened. They suggested I let her go to the Cities because if I did not, she would probably cause trouble all weekend. She got her way again. She then told them she wanted to go live with her father. By this time, I had no objections to that idea. They wanted me to call him and make the arrangements myself, but I knew if I asked him, the answer would be no. I asked Social Services to make the arrangements because he would not turn them down. They did and he agreed to give it a try. As soon as she came home from the Cities, she was to go live with him. He called me that weekend and tried to pull out of doing this. He wanted to try having her for two weeks. I said no, I would not take her back for at least three months, preferably six months. Then he started putting off the day she was to move in. On Monday morning, I called Social Services and told them what he was doing and asked them to handle it.

I sat Michelle down and told her that she was not going to play a game between her father and me. If she decided in the future she wanted to come home, she had better be positive about that because I would only take her back once. She could not come home because she was not getting her way at her father's and then go to his house when she did not get her way here. By the middle of that week, she was living with her father, his girlfriend, and her children. Then Elizabeth told me that her sister had all of this planned long before we went on our Florida trip. She did not want to miss out on the trip, so she waited to do this until after our trip!

Thirteen days later, Michelle called me sobbing. Her father said she had to move out because things were not going well. He was going to make her live with friends of his if I would not take her home. She wanted to come home. I told her I needed to talk it over with her stepfather and her sister first. To say the least, none of us were excited about the prospect, but we decided perhaps she had learned that the grass is not always greener on the other side of the fence. I told her that in order for us to let her come home, she had to follow the rules and quit insisting on getting her way all the time. She needed to make a real effort to treat her sister and my husband better than she had been. She agreed and I allowed her to move back home.

What my daughter had done was take the power that our government has given to our children and then used it in an inappropriate way to get what she wanted. She had no idea that along with power comes responsibility. She began to learn she had to take responsibility for her actions. She was pretty mellow for a long time after she came home. The two girls were distant in their relationship now and we moved Michelle down into one of the bedrooms in the basement so that they each had privacy. I noticed that whenever I left the house for any reason at all, my husband left right behind me. I asked him what that was all about. He told me he thought he had better protect himself! Since Michelle had called Social Services on me for no reason, he figured she was capable of doing the same to him. She still made it clear she did not like my husband and would occasionally try to cause trouble between us. He refused to be in a position where he would ever be alone with her. It was terribly sad to me that he felt this way, but I did not blame him one bit.

Elizabeth learned by watching what her brother and sisters were going through and decided she was not going to take their routes. The only thing I was concerned about with her was the fact that she did not talk about her feelings. She kept them all inside. If I asked her what was wrong when she was obviously unhappy, her response was, "Nothing." If I tried to press her about it, she would become agitated and go to her room.

Ed was stationed in Hawaii. In June of 1987, I received a call from him. He was in California and did not have enough money to get back to Mankato, could I wire him some? Since he had said nothing to me in his letters or phone calls about an upcoming leave, I thought this was strange. If he was in trouble again, I did not want to be a part of it so I told him I couldn't send him any money. A week later, he was living back in Mankato. He came to our house quite often and our relationship was improving. He began to understand some of the things he needed to look at and deal with. He went back to the program and began working through his issues. When it became too hard for him to continue, he used again for short periods of time.

I worked with my husband during the summer. We went camping with the kids and our friends as often as we could. He and I made sure we spent our own special time together every day. Our relationship was strong, loving, and fun. We were strong in our respective programs and went to as many regional roundups as we could besides our weekly meetings. We both grew in knowledge and stamina to handle the problems we faced. We were involved in Bible studies and had many good friends in our lives which we spent time with on a regular basis.

In September I received a phone call from the police. They were looking for Ed. I asked why and they said the Army was looking for him because he was AWOL. I told them Ed was in Mankato, but I did not have an address or a phone number for him because he had not given me that information. He was picked up two weeks later. He had a hearing in October and was released from the Army.

Chapter 8 - Revelation and Resolve

41 Feelings of Abandonment Manifested

Marie got married in November of 1987. The following year, 1988, Emery married in March, and Omar married in May. At the end of May, my husband and I went to a roundup in the Cities and Marie was at home with the girls. We received a phone call from her on Saturday. Michelle had run away during the night and Marie did not know what she should do. She knew where her sister was, however, so we told her to do nothing. I told Marie that Michelle was not going to spoil our weekend. If the police brought Michelle home for Marie to deal with, Marie might regret it. By the time we came home the next day, our runaway was home. I grounded her, which did absolutely no good because she snuck out whenever she wanted to.

We went camping during the summer and this time Michelle continued her angry fits even while camping. We sent her to Bible Camp for two weeks which was a needed break for all of us. She came home from camp excited about her experience. As she shared it with us, it sounded as if she experienced a spiritual awakening. She behaved differently toward all of us. She tried hard to not fight with Elizabeth. She talked more about her feelings, dreams, and aspirations. This new attitude and behavior lasted for a couple of months, which was a wonderful respite from the way things had been before she went to camp.

In July of 1988, Marie's marriage ended. Her husband had been physically abusing her and she finally had enough. We moved her and our five-month-old granddaughter home with us. Marie had a full-time job but could not afford daycare and still get on her feet. We decided I could quit working with my husband for the winter and take care of our granddaughter and a couple of the neighbor kids. Michelle resented this because she could no longer have my full attention all of the time. My husband and our granddaughter became very close. He played with her a lot and everyday they went into his office, sat together and watched "Fraggle Rock." She loved this so much that she sat still with her "Papa" for the entire half-hour show. By the time she was one, when we asked her, "Who's the greatest?", she would say "Papa!" On December 1, 1988, Marie moved into her own apartment. I continued to baby-sit for our granddaughter for the rest of the winter.

Since Elizabeth had gymnastics to keep her busy, we decided Michelle needed something to do which would interest her and hopefully keep her out of trouble. I heard that kids with low self-esteem did very well after being in Tae Kwon Do. We asked her if she wanted to take lessons and she did, so I enrolled her for three months. She enjoyed it very much and it gave her more self-confidence. She began to do better in school. We had been watching Elizabeth at her gymnastic meets and now we would go to watch Michelle perform exhibitions in Tae Kwon Do. She was excellent and very dedicated to what she was learning. She earned her brown belt in a matter of weeks.

In February of 1989, I received a call from the mother of one of Michelle's friends. Michelle was at her house and had taken a lot of pills on top of alcohol. She had tried to commit suicide! With the help of a police officer, I took her to the hospital. I did not understand why this was happening, and I was scared for my daughter. On the way home from the hospital, I began to wonder if sobriety and all the work I had done on myself was really worth it; the problems just kept coming. The program promised that if I did what I was supposed to, there would be rewards. Since I stopped drinking, it seemed like things with the children got worse instead of better. The program also told me God would not give me more than I could handle. I wondered how much He thought I could handle, because I felt I had reached my limit. I felt weak and vulnerable. I needed strength, so I began to pray the third step prayer from the book of Alcoholics Anonymous: "God, I offer myself to Thee–to build with me and to do with me as Thou wilt. Relieve me of the bondage of self, that I may better do Thy will. Take away my difficulties, that victory over them may bear witness to those I would help of Thy Power, Thy Love, and Thy Way of life. May I do Thy will always!"[3]

When I went to see Michelle the next day, I sat and talked to the nurses for a long time and asked if they knew what this was all about. They could not tell me without my daughter's permission. How was I to help my child if I did not know what was wrong? They gave me ever-so-subtle hints so I could figure it out. I went home and my husband and I sat down and tried to think of something, anything, that might have caused her to do this. While we were talking, a terrible feeling took over my stomach, and thoughts kept going through my head about her nightmares and bedwetting when she was young. I called Marie and asked her to come over to help me figure out what had happened to her sister in 1977 and 1978. We talked about possible sexual abuse, but by whom? The only people we could remember her being alone with were her grandfather and her father. Her grandfather was not capable of such a thing, and even though her father had treated me very abusively, he had always treated the children very well. But there wasn't anyone else with whom she had been alone during that time. At that moment, Elizabeth, who had been standing out of sight in the kitchen doorway, came running into the room with tears streaming down her face and said, "It wasn't Dad, it was the baby-sitter." Marie and I looked at each other in shock, and we both asked, "What baby-sitter?" She told us the name of the young man who sat for them during that time. Now things were beginning to make sense, and I felt sick inside. Why hadn't I listened to my gut feelings at that time and done something about what I thought and felt? I went to see Michelle the next day and told her that I knew what had happened to her. She glared at me with such anger and hatred that it was hard for me to continue talking to her. I told her I did not blame her for being angry with me; she felt abandoned by me when this happened to her and from then on, she did not trust me to protect her. I told her I knew how that felt and I would do whatever she needed me to do to help her get better and for us to work through this together. This was the beginning of a very long and painful recovery process for both of us.

We placed her into Willow Street which is an adolescent treatment center in Minneapolis for emotionally disturbed children. For the next three months, Elizabeth, my husband, and I drove up every week for counseling with her. She had felt abandoned by her father and me for a long time. I called her father and met with him to let him know what was going on. I begged him to be involved in her counseling as she needed him now as much as she needed me. For whatever reasons, he chose to not be involved. My husband and I did all we could to make sure she did not feel abandoned again.

My husband went to all the counseling sessions, staffings, and parent groups, even when she acted as though she did not want him there. Her treatment of him in the past made sense now. She periodically allowed herself to get close to him and then would be mean to him in order to push him away because she was afraid he would eventually abandon her. Family therapy with her was intense and painful. There were times I felt we were getting nowhere. I wondered if she and I could ever have a relationship of any kind. I mourned the loss of the wonderful free spirit she had been before she was five. The guilt I felt for having failed her sometimes was so intense that I could hardly function. I wanted to be able to take her pain away, and I felt helpless and inadequate.

When her time at Willow Street was nearing an end, we had to decide whether to have her come home or go to a foster home. Elizabeth was adamant in that she didn't want her sister to come home. She had no desire to have our home life return to what it had been before and did not trust that her sister had changed enough. Elizabeth had received our full attention while Michelle was in the hospital and did not have to worry about her personal things being taken by her sister. Our home life was serene and peaceful. This was the first time I saw Elizabeth be assertive and I knew she meant what she said. As it turned out, the treatment facility convinced Michelle to go to a foster home for six months, and continue family counseling before gradually moving back home. We found a wonderful psychologist whom we all trusted and we finally made progress as she did not allow us to skirt around the real issues. She helped us each to own up to our individual responsibilities in our relationships with other family members. In a matter of months, our family was on a healthier road to communicating better with each other. She helped each of us set healthy boundaries for ourselves and to gain confidence in ourselves in order to not allow any family member to step over those boundaries. She helped me believe I had done all I could do to help Michelle and now the rest of Michelle's healing was her own responsibility.

While Michelle was in foster care, our girls started to communicate with each other as sisters on a more normal level. They were being quite cautious because they had both hurt each other in the past. My relationship with Elizabeth was getting better. She sometimes talked to me about her feelings and I knew we were making progress. She was beginning to trust that she would not be pushed aside again. Through all that had gone on, she excelled in everything she did and she did it all on her own. She was kind, considerate, respectful, funny, even-tempered, helpful, and a "people pleaser." She took care of everyone else's needs and wants, and put her own needs and wants aside. I knew this had to change. I worried she believed that she was not important or worthwhile. She would not talk about this so all I could do was to keep my eyes and ears open when she talked about what she liked and wished to do. I saw to it the best I could that her needs and wants were met.

I stopped daycare when school let out in May of 1989 and worked with my husband. Elizabeth baby-sat for her niece during this summer while Marie worked. We camped whenever we could and Michelle came home on weekends.

By the end of October, we all agreed to have Michelle come back home to live.

Elizabeth won many first place ribbons during all the regular gymnastic meets that fall and she advanced to the state tournaments which were to be held in March of 1990.

42 Detaching with Love

On January 12, 1990, I received a phone call from the St. Peter Police. Michelle was found behind a restaurant so terribly intoxicated that she could not stand up. They wanted me to come and get her. I told them to do what they normally did when they found people this way. They said they normally put them in Detox, so I told them to take her to Detox. Because she was a minor, I had to sign a release in order for them to take her. From Detox, Social Services and I put her into Chemical Dependency Treatment. She was court-ordered to three months of treatment. After treatment, she was court-ordered to go to a youth group home for six months. While she was there, we again went to counseling with her. She came home on weekends and gradually our relationship grew into a healthy and close one.

In March, Elizabeth won first place in Vault, second place in Floor Exercise, second place on the Balance Beam, and second place on the Bars at the State Gymnastics Tournaments. We went with her to the Cities for the weekend and had a wonderful time watching her perform. She had worked very hard to accomplish all of this and we were grateful to be a part of her celebration.

In July, Michelle came home from the group home. I was glad to have her home. We were now able to share a lot with each other. It was during this time I asked her why she had not told me about the molestation. She told me that when she was seven, she told the boy's mother and was called a liar. Due to that, she did not think anyone else would believe her.

Michelle turned eighteen in August and moved to St. Peter to repeat her senior year of high school. She moved in with two of her friends for a few months and then rented her own apartment. She did quite well considering she was living on about two hundred dollars a month and going to school full-time. She grew up very quickly during this period of time. Her attitude toward the family changed dramatically. She came home on the weekends and we sometimes talked into the wee hours of the morning. She and her younger sister became buddies and she began to treat her step-dad better.

During the following winter, I discovered that Elizabeth had not been able to cope with all that happened as well as we thought she had. It was still difficult for her to express her feelings to anyone. She did not want to hurt anyone. Marie found out she was suffering from an eating disorder and relayed this information to me. When I confronted Elizabeth, she became quite angry. She felt we had invaded her privacy. She told me she had already started to go to a support group, which was helping, and she was seeing the school counselor. I was relieved and pleased that she took it upon herself to get help. Since she recognized her problem and had taken steps to help herself, I backed off and let her handle it. Every once in a while, she let me know she was making progress. A year later, she no longer struggled with it.

Marie married again in December of 1990. She was sober now and on the road to a new life.

Ed married in January of 1991. He had been in the program and sober for a year and he was growing and changing by leaps and bounds.

At this time, Michelle had a miscarriage and was absolutely devastated by it even though she realized it was for the best. All I could do was listen to her when she needed to talk about how she felt, hold her when she cried, and let her stay at home when she did not want to be alone. During the next couple of months, she and I formed a relationship that I never would have believed possible. It seemed there was nothing we couldn't talk about. This is what I had prayed for. Perhaps after all these years of hard work, she would finally be okay. It was so wonderful to be able to talk and laugh with her.

In March of 1991, we went to the State Gymnastics Tournament with Elizabeth. Her knees and ankles bothered her quite a bit by this time, yet she did very well in the tournaments and won several ribbons. Afterward, she went to an orthopedic surgeon, who told her that if she chose to continue in gymnastics, she would need surgery on her knees before too long. She quit taking lessons and was hired by her studio to teach gymnastics. I thought that was a wise decision for her to make. She was an excellent teacher and it helped her to continue the friendships she had acquired in the gymnastics club.

In April, Michelle moved home because she could not stand living alone, and the manager of her apartment building had been sexually harassing both she and a friend. She commuted back and forth to school in St. Peter. At the end of the school year, she still needed a few credits in order to graduate. At the invitation of a friend's family, she moved to Staples, Minnesota, to stay with this family in order to finish her education during the summer. It had been wonderful having her home for a little while and I hated to see her go. In August, she turned nineteen and graduated from high school. I admired the fact that she stuck with it and did whatever it took to graduate, especially since school had been difficult for her.

She came home and found a job at the River Hills Mall. Shortly thereafter, she began to date a young man from St. Peter whom she had met while in school there. We all liked him very much. The two of them seemed to be good for each other and she was very happy. She lived at home the rest of 1991. It looked like our family was finally coming together. Things were still a bit tense between Michelle and her step-dad, but they were getting along better than ever before. The two of them could actually talk and even laugh together once in a while. The girls were getting along well and my relationship with both girls was good.

Ed and his wife were no longer in the program. He was convinced all he needed was church. After doing as well as he had, all of us in the family, and those who knew him well, ached for him because we knew what was bound to happen next. It was not long before he was using again. It was painful to see him having such a difficult time. Our relationship deteriorated again to nonexistent in short order.

During this time, I noticed Marie had an awful lot of resentment about her growing up years and she expressed jealousy toward both of her sisters. She and I began to talk about how she was feeling and all she believed she had missed out on. It has been a slow process for us to heal our relationship so that we can be comfortable with one another. As long as we both continue to work our programs, we will be able to get through the issues and our relationship will continue to grow and improve.

43 Rewards

In September of 1991, my husband and I took a weekend

trip to Duluth. In our spontaneity, we drove up there without making reservations anywhere. We discovered when we began to look for somewhere to stay that perhaps we had made a big mistake. It took us a while, but we did find a room about seven miles out of town. It was great to get away by ourselves. We drove up the North Shore and toured a number of places along the way. We went to a fantastic park with seven water falls. We walked along the waterfront in Duluth and found a great sports bar in which to have dinner. The bar had an indoor volleyball court and we watched a game being played while we ate. It was a fun and relaxing weekend for us. We came home rested and rejuvenated.

By February of 1992, Michelle spent most of her time with her boyfriend at his parents' home. She came home once in a while to get clean clothes, to visit, and for dinner.

I had been working in a drugstore since August of 1990 because work in our business is pretty sparse during the winter. This job helped us financially and I enjoyed working there. I was now the Pharmacy Technician. One of the other drugstores in town went out of business and we took on their clientele. The work load became horrendous and by May, I was burned out. I gave my resignation to my boss and could hardly wait to get out of the Pharmacy. I could work with my husband again! I had missed working with him and being with him.

Elizabeth, my husband, and I worked together all summer and it was great. We took a week off and went to the Wisconsin Dells with Elizabeth and a friend of hers. While there, we experienced our first helicopter ride. Elizabeth and her friend went bungie jumping, but I chickened out. We took a ride on the Duck Boats which are designed for all terrains.

Part of the ride was through very rough and hilly terrain which got us down to the river. Then we rode on the river for a while and then back onto land. It was great fun. We saw a water-ski show which was spectacular. My husband and I took a Riverboat Tour along the Dells while the girls found better things to do in town. On the way home, we drove to Winona to see Omar and his family. We stayed overnight in a motel and took the kids to Garvin Heights, which is a lookout point on top of one of the high cliffs surrounding Winona. From there, one can see all of Winona below and many miles of the Mississippi River Valley.

Michelle and her friend moved to Willmar because they were both going to go to college there. He found a job at the Community Center and she went to school. By the end of July, they were expecting a baby. They were going to wait to get married until after the baby was born, but in September, they decided they wanted to be married before the birth of their child. They asked if we would give them a small church wedding and we said yes. We only had a month to put this wedding together, but I had a wonderful time because of how easily they were satisfied with what we could afford to do. The more appreciative they were, the more we wanted to do for them. On October 24, 1992, they were married.

My husband began to make a cradle for our new grandchild-not-yet-born. Michelle had been fascinated with cloud formations ever since she was little so he made the cradle to look like a cloud. She was thrilled when he gave it to her. She and her husband moved back to St. Peter in December because they were both very homesick and did not like Willmar. In early February, 1993, Michelle's sisters and I were at the hospital with them waiting for their baby to be born. We walked the halls with her, making her laugh throughout her contractions. I don't know what she would tell you about that day, but we had a great time!

During the summer of 1993, I was privileged to go on a week's vacation with my mother and sister. We had not been able to do that before and I was quite nervous about it. I hoped my sister and I would be able to spend the week getting much closer than we had been. She is a very private person. Because of that, it has been difficult for me to feel closely connected to her. During this week, we were given the opportunity to talk about many things we had not talked about before.

I enjoyed being with my mother during this week and was able to resolve one more issue with her during the week. Although she and I get on each other's nerves occasionally, (as do all mothers and daughters), she and I talk through our problems with each other and resolve them. I feel close to her and love her dearly.

Ed's marriage ended the summer of 1993. While he was going through the breakup of his marriage, he came home often and we were able to put our relationship on the road to healing once again. He moved to Colorado in the fall. He has talked about living out there since he was ten years old. We talk to him often and he has been back in the program since December and has continued with his church. We have heard the difference in him and his attitude since then. We hope and pray he will commit himself to the program this time so he can finally heal.

All of our children are doing well and working hard to be the people they were meant to be. They all know life is a process and change is inevitable.

It is now May of 1994 and we have been blessed with

seven grandchildren who have brought much joy into our lives. It is truly a blessing to be able to watch them grow. We acquired one of our seven grandchildren through Marie's marriage.

Marie and her husband have both been sober and in the program for almost five years. They have struggled because so much growing and so many changes take place within each of us during sobriety. They are both good people. I have to believe and pray they will get through their trials. Marie and I have had problems communicating with each other in the past, and it seems to have a direct connection to where we are at in each of our programs at the time. We keep working on it and loving each other. I know it will get better in time. Marie has worked very hard on herself, particularly in the last six months, and is growing out of some past painful issues because she is ready to resolve them.

Michelle and I have a beautiful relationship. There is nothing that we cannot talk about. The relationship between she and my husband has changed dramatically. They talk and laugh together and she loves watching him play with her daughter. A year and a half ago, she thanked us for our sobriety. She realized how lucky she was that for the past fourteen years she has had sober parents. She told us she has friends whose parents use drugs and alcohol all of the time and she could not imagine having to live that way.

Elizabeth graduates from high school this year. It has been an absolute joy to see her grow. She is a compassionate, loving, and caring person. She loves life and all the possibilities it has to offer. She has grown from a shy, introverted girl into an outgoing, fun-loving, assertive young lady. She knows where she wants to go in life and she knows what she has to do to get there. She has done well in school throughout her education and she is a National Honor Society student. The past two years, she was on her school's diving team and excelled there as well. This past year, my husband and I attended her diving meets and enjoyed watching her and cheering for her. I could see the pride he has in her. She is taking a trip to Hawaii the day after graduation, and in the fall she will be attending Winona State University. Her goal is to be a Registered Nurse.

Emery and his wife are fun people. They are free spirits and love the outdoors. They do a lot of camping and hiking. Since they have no children, they pick up and go wherever they choose. My husband and I went camping with them for a weekend two years ago and had a great time. It is always fun when we get together with them.

Omar and his wife are also wonderful people. They have so many different interests and are very knowledgeable about many things. I have never been bored when we have been together. We see them on some of the holidays and three or four times a year.

We are proud of all of our children and our sons- and daughters-in-law. They are all loving, caring, kind, hard-working, compassionate, respectful, and spiritual people.

When my husband and I were married in 1984, we never dreamed what lay ahead of us. To look back, we know we were given strength by God to not only deal with all that faced us, but also to keep us all together. We both started our marriage with faith in God that He would help us in whatever we faced together. We did what we needed to do for ourselves by continually going to our meetings in the program. That helped us grow in our spirituality. It helped each of us to change the things we needed to change within ourselves so we could grow together. It gave us a place to talk about what went on in our lives and get suggestions and ideas of how to handle them.

We talked to each other and decided together what to do in situations. Then we supported each other in those decisions. We availed ourselves of all the help we could find. We made sure that we went away together for a few days at a time without the children to spend time with each other and our friends. We saw to it that we spent time visiting with our parents, our grown children, and our grandchildren. When we were tempted to quit, we prayed for strength to continue, and it always came. We did not give up on God, each other, or our children.

In our marriage, there has not been one day when we have forgotten to hug and kiss each other. Each and every day of our marriage we have told each other, "I love you." My husband has not once criticized me or put me down in any way. He has supported me in everything I have chosen to do. If what I try does not work out, he just says it was good I tried it anyway. He has been there for the children, and willingly participated in all that needed to be done. He allows me the time and space to grow and change at my own pace. He accepts me just the way I am. Every day he teaches me what love really is by the way he loves me, and giving to me and others without thought of return or expectations. We do not fight because we talk things through until we reach an understanding, compromise, or acceptance. We work together in everything and we have fun together. Whenever we walk anywhere together, he takes my hand. I wish for everyone to feel as loved as I feel.

Planting the seed of a child and giving birth are biological acts. In order to be a mother or a father, there must be unconditional love and commitment toward the child; to nurture, teach, support, guide, and always have the health and welfare of the child at heart. My husband has truly been a father to my children.

There have been no major crises in our lives in the past three years and life is good. Calm is something I have definitely learned to appreciate. We celebrated our tenth anniversary this past March and are looking forward to the next ten years.

3. *Alcoholics Anonymous* (Alcoholics Anonymous World Services, Inc., 1939) p. 63.

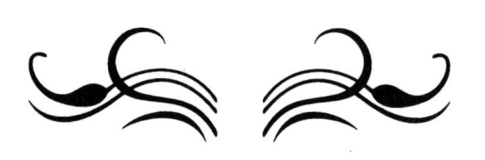

In Summary

The abuse we suffer as children often takes the rest of our lives to overcome. We, as individuals and as a society, need to understand that as long as we allow abuse to go on, we will have a violent society. We need to teach our children early in life that to love and to be loved is not supposed to hurt. To love means to encourage individuality, to teach acceptance and respect of others, to guide in the making of decisions, and to teach individual responsibilities.

In their zeal to stop child abuse, our government and our court systems have given our children power which they do not know how to handle. The power the children have received is power without responsibility. Children need boundaries and to be held responsible for their behavior. We have to stop allowing individuals to blame their behavior on someone else. No matter what has happened to us, we need to take responsibility for our own lives and our own behavior.

I began my recovery and healing when I entered the twelve-step program I have mentioned many times in my story. It is a program of individual responsibility. All the counseling which I had before entering the program did not help me recover or heal. Instead, it allowed me to continue to blame others, feel sorry for myself, and keep myself sedated. Healing will not take place that way.

There were times in my life I wished I was someone else and lived a different life. I no longer have those wishes. What matters is not so much the hand I was dealt, but what I chose to do with it. Through the many mistakes I made, I learned and changed. Today I am a person of strength and resolve. I no longer feel like a victim because I no longer allow people to victimize me. I like who I am today. I also believe that in each stage of my life, I did the best I could with what I knew. I am proud of the work I have done on myself in my program. There have been many miracles in my life. I am grateful to my Heavenly Father for being with me from the very beginning. I used to be so angry with Him for allowing terrible things to happen to me. When I learned what love really is, I understood that He is not in the business of controlling anyone's behavior. If He was, we would all be robots. He gives each of us the strength to get through what others do to us and we do to ourselves. He puts people in our path to help us and we are the ones who either accept or reject His help. The amazing thing is that no matter how often I pushed Him away, He always gave me another chance to turn my life around so I could get close to Him. Today I count on Him each and every day to be by my side and guide me to do His will.

To the best of my ability, I live by practicing the principles of my program in all my affairs, by the principles set down for us in the Book of Proverbs, and by having conscious contact with my Lord and Savior Jesus Christ each and every day.

I consciously make the effort to continue to grow emotionally and spiritually. I am better than I was, but I am nowhere near where I want to be. Today I welcome working through my character defects and shortcomings in order to be the person God meant for me to be.

I believe we all have a responsibility to each other. We

need to help each other through life's journey whenever we can. We were not put on Earth to go through life alone. We need to connect with each other. If we choose to do that, perhaps then we will begin to heal ourselves and our society. We need to do whatever we can to stop all kinds of abuse, whenever and wherever we find it. Each and every one of us needs to be responsible to act in defense of the defenseless. To do less makes us a part of the problem instead of a part of the solution.

I wish for you the strength and willingness to look at your life and yourself so that you, too, can heal your wounds and be healthy, serene, and happy. You won't have to do it alone. God will be with you every step of the way.